THE AIRGUNNER'S COMPANION

THE AIRGUNNER'S COMPANION

A Field Guide to Hunting with Air Rifles

J D J Braithwaite

Quiller

DEDICATION

To my wife, Katty, whom I love with all my heart and apologise to sincerely for all the hours spent away from her in the forests, fells, and fields of the Lake District.

Copyright © 2019 J D J Braithwaite

First published in the UK in 2019
by Quiller, an imprint of Quiller Publishing Ltd

British Library Cataloguing-in-Publication Data
A catalogue record for this book is available from
the British Library

ISBN 978 1 84689 3018

All rights reserved. No part of this book may be reproduced or transmitted in any form or by any means, electronic or mechanical including photocopying, recording or by any information storage and retrieval system, without permission from the Publisher in writing.

Edited by Rosie Barham

Printed in the Czech Republic

Whilst every effort has been made to obtain permission from copyright holders for all material used in this book, the publishers will be pleased to hear from anyone who has not been appropriately acknowledged, and to make the correction in future reprints.

It is important that readers should abide by, and be familiar with, the legal requirements concerning the control of avian and vermin species within their territory of activity.

Quiller
An imprint of Quiller Publishing Ltd
Wykey House, Wykey, Shrewsbury SY4 1JA
Tel: 01939 261616
Email: info@quillerbooks.com
Website: www.quillerpublishing.com

Contents

1 INTRODUCTION
My background _____ 9
Airgunning and me _____ 10

2 WHY CHOOSE AN AIRGUN?
The 'good ole days' of airgunning _____ 15
The philosophy of the airgun hunter _____ 16
Advantages of the airgun _____ 17
The frustration of hunting with airguns _____ 18
Hunting with airguns: It's not for the faint-hearted _____ 19
Airguns in the 21st century _____ 20
Airguns: Myths and misconceptions _____ 21

3 GETTING STARTED
Know the law: Airguns, vermin, and general licences _____ 24
Associations that support airgunners _____ 26
Learn about wildlife species _____ 26
Spring-powered and Pre-Charged Pneumatic (PCP) airguns _____ 27
Buying an airgun for hunting _____ 30
Which calibre for hunting? _____ 35
Establishing the sweet-spot (PCPs) _____ 37
Custom and tuned air rifles _____ 39
The best pellets for hunting _____ 43
Telescopic sights (scopes) _____ 48
Sound moderators _____ 51
Getting to know your combination _____ 53
Zeroing your rifle for optimal performance _____ 56
My own hunting combinations _____ 62
Point of impact (POI) on live quarry _____ 70

THE AIRGUNNER'S COMPANION

The importance of continued target practice	76
Shooting technique: Some basic tips	76

4 HUNTING: PERMISSIONS

Gaining permissions	79
Shared permissions	80
Listen to the landowner	81
Doing your research: Assess the challenges posed by the land	81
Develop a strategy	82
Shooting alone or with partners	83

5 HUNTING: EQUIPMENT

Getting serious	84
Knives and knife-sharpening kits	84
Shooting sticks and bipods	87
Shooting seats	89
Rucksacks and backpacks	90
Laser rangefinders	91
Lamping kits and night vision	91
Thermal spotters	93
Camouflage and hunting apparel	93
Footwear	98
Camo-netting and hides	99
Wildlife, trail and surveillance cameras	101
Decoys (deeks)	102
A big freezer	103
Miscellaneous items	103

6 HUNTING: FIELDCRAFT

The importance of fieldcraft	105
Observation	105
How to use your camouflage and environment effectively	107
Stalking	115
The art of ambushing	120
Hunting in woodlands	123

CONTENTS

Shooting around the farmyard	128
Lamping	130
Feeding and baiting	133
An optimised feeder-based approach	134
Decoying	146
Use a broken rhythm	148
Handling culled animals	150

7 HUNTING: FUR
Rabbits, grey squirrel, wild mink, rats 153

8 HUNTING: FEATHER
Woodpigeons, collared doves, feral pigeons 169
Corvids: blue-jays, magpies, crows, rooks and jackdaws 172

9 HUNTING: THINGS TO CONSIDER ON EVERY TRIP
Challenging weather and wind conditions 179
Distance to target 181
Incline and decline 181
Checking the zero 183

10 CASE STUDIES
Some of my own hunting and conservation projects 184
Stately Estate (I): Squirrel project 184
Stately Estate (I): Rabbits 188
Woodland: Grey squirrels, rats 190
Farm (I): Rabbits 194
Farm (II): Rabbits 196
Stately Estate (II): Rabbits and grey squirrels 198
A farewell, thank you and happy hunting 199

ACKNOWLEDGEMENTS 201

INDEX 203

1 INTRODUCTION

MY BACKGROUND

I was born and raised in the western Lake District region of Cumbria. Generations of my family have lived in the region, going back hundreds of years – specifically the Eskdale, Wasdale, Ravenglass, Corney, and Bootle village areas – so it is a place I can call home. My late and ever-colourful grandfather was a true Dalesman and a master of many field sports, most notably salmon fishing in the River Esk, that gives the Eskdale valley its name. Field sports, the country ways, and shooting have always been a part of my life.

When I left school at 16 years old, I got an apprenticeship as an engineer in a local, well-respected establishment, but my real passion was science. After a few years as an engineer, and taking the time to complete my A-levels at night school, I left for university and graduated with a BSc (Hons) degree in 1999. I then won a scholarship for a PhD, which I completed in 2002. I am now an academic and I bring these skills to my approach toward hunting.

To some it might seem odd to be a scientist and into airgunning. These might not appear to be typical bedfellows, but to my mind this says more about the prejudices of others than my legitimate passion for the sport. I shoot with airguns in my spare time as much as I can, which sadly, is never enough to feed my passion. I have a number of shooting projects in Cumbria, and I am privileged to have the trust and respect of the landowners who allow me to shoot over their land, and to be a part of important conservation projects, like protecting the red squirrel population by culling grey squirrels, or hunting the rabbits that eat expensive plants on stately estates.

I am rarely happier than when I am alone in the middle of vast woodland, being close to nature on a summer or autumn evening. There is nothing quite like watching the sun go down whilst you learn from what is happening around you. In this modern world of ever-demanding jobs, computerised games machines, the Internet, and 24-hour television, few people ever experience a true connection to the rawness of the wild. Being in the middle of British woodland, unaccompanied

THE AIRGUNNER'S COMPANION

by the irritating sounds of traffic, bleating car or house alarms, not even the sounds of human voices softened by the distance, is an important and much cherished part of my life.

When hunting, I swap the drone of everyday experience for being surrounded by birdsong; cuckoo calls, the 'coo' of woodpigeons, pheasant barks, blackbird trills; the tranquil sound of flowing streams, the wind blowing through the tree canopy, the smell of wet grass, and clean air in my face, which in the autumn and winter months is sufficient to turn my nose and ears numb; magnificent skies and fabulous sunsets revealing a riot of colour from the Lakeland woodland and fells. It is also to experience true darkness away from all artificial lighting, where you cannot see your own hand two feet from your face.

Airgunning has brought me closer to nature than I ever could be by other means. It has enriched my life in ways that I never anticipated, for which I am deeply grateful. Growing up in Lakeland has led to my understanding of the countryside being both healthy and realistic. I believe I am a better person for it, although I suppose that is for others to judge. My mind has been educated about our wildlife, and I am constantly learning new things. I hope, in my own way, that I've made a contribution toward managing the wildlife for the betterment of it.

Experienced airgunners will know what I mean when I say, 'you do not have to shoot anything on a hunting trip to enjoy yourself and be enriched by the experience of being out there in the countryside, feeling you are a part of it'. Inexperienced airgunners can look forward to finding out just what I mean. Your enjoyment is not measured by the size of your quarry bag, but a full bag is a special feeling of a job well done. You never master the airgun, or hunting with it, but the journey of trying to master it brings great enjoyment. It is about the journey, not the destination. Happy travelling!

AIRGUNNING AND ME

In his youth, my father had shotguns and shot crows from the back of tractors ploughing fields, or bunnies fleeing from his ferrets in the Eskdale valley in the late 1940s and early 1950s. He then went on to have a Fire Arms Certificate (FAC) .22 rifle. When we kids were growing up, he got rid of his guns for fear of safety issues with us running about the house. Later on, he got an air rifle.

INTRODUCTION

Airgunning can bring you close to nature and the countryside as well as providing you with priceless moments like this one. Returning after a day's woodland shooting I was greeted by a glorious view and sunset on the walk back to the car.

At this time, he worked for the Ministry of Defence, as a security guard on a military testing range, and often took the gun into work to shoot at night. I'll always remember him coming home with bags full of rabbits, and as a small child I would sit with him to watch him gut, skin and butcher the bunnies in our kitchen; he would give me the rabbit tails to play with. He picked up on my early fascination and curiosity and explained to me the concepts, and need for vermin and pest control, as well as the importance of respect for the animal. He was so proficient at airgunning that neighbours would come to the door and ask if he had any spare from time to time, or put their orders in for him. Everyone knew he nearly always had rabbits and he shared them freely.

Growing up, we ate well. Many in the *real* countryside did. Indeed, when my father was a small child growing up during the war, he always stated that he was never aware of rations. In the countryside, there always seemed to be a salmon, rabbit, pigeon, duck, or pheasant on the table. When he had been very successful he would walk around Eskdale giving the local families and the elderly spare rabbits to ensure that they did not go without provisions during this challenging period.

THE AIRGUNNER'S COMPANION

I started practising seriously with airguns in my youth (early 1980s), sitting on the cold ground in the family back garden with my father's .22 Webley Vulcan and tins of terrible Hustler pellets – they were the only brand we could get hold of back then. I learned my craft by spending hours shooting at spoon heads, clothes pegs – my late mother was furious! – old toy action-man figures, and jam-jar lids. I washed the neighbours' cars, worked as a bottling-up boy at the local pub, and helped farmers during hay-time, and nearly all my earnings went on tins of pellets or new parts for the Vulcan, which like all of us, aged far too quickly.

My father told me that I needed to be able to get pellet groupings – say 7 or 8 shots out of 10 – no bigger in spread than the diameter of a two-pence piece, at 25 yards, before he would let me take on any culling of live quarry. To do otherwise would be inhumane, he said, and these were wise words. This was also in the days of open-barrel sights and the Vulcan kicked like a mule, so trust me when I say this was harder than it sounds. It took me a long time to get to that level, but it slowly happened and then I was ready.

I have many happy memories of those early days. I remember adding white chalk to the fore sight on the barrel so I could see it at dusk and continue practising, rather than having to pack up, go into the house, and take an early bath for school the next day. I remember buying my first telescopic sight – second-hand, of course – a 4x15mm scope, followed up with a 4x20mm wide-angle scope, which in a rather endearing way had a slightly bent lateral line just to the right of the central crosshair. It also required constant re-zeroing because it would creep due to the recoiling airgun.

All this was paid for by whatever money I could make outside of school hours. The scopes extended my range, and made me better at the ones I had already practised; my father made good use of the new glassware on the gun and the bunny count increased even more. Homework suffered, and I am sure that was one reason it took me a few years of being an engineer before I actually got to university. At this time in my life, the call of the woods was stronger than that of the library.

Back then, airgunning was so basic, so primitive, and yet so devastatingly effective. That Webley Vulcan was an absolute killing machine in my father's hands. Before leaving school I got a good summer job working on a farm. The work was hard and the hours were long, but the pay was very good, even by today's standards. With a friend, we also got our first formal shooting permission from another local farmer. His land was riddled with rabbits and rats, among an array of other legal vermin. However, the now ageing Vulcan was no longer really up to the job. This

INTRODUCTION

project and my growing interest in airgunning required something more effective, so I saved for a new MK II Weihrauch HW80 in .22 calibre. A friend loaned me a 3–9 x 40mm scope and I was in business. At the same time, he got a new Theoben Sirocco when they were a very new and innovative design – lovely gun. These were happy days indeed.

This was in the late 1980s, and at that time, two airguns were legendary and most people involved in serious vermin control either owned, or had owned them. They were both Weihrauchs (HWs) – namely, the under-lever HW77 and the break-barrel HW80. With the HW80 I knew I had a serious bit of kit, and no excuses for lame performance in the field. We bagged enough to learn our trade and provide a basic service for the farmer. I also shot a wild mink on this land with the HW80, and it was one of the most satisfying shots I've ever taken. I will never forget it. From a standing position, a clean head shot, instantly dead, sent spinning from a tree in corkscrew fashion from about 25 yards – mink have small heads! Don't believe the rumours that there are no mink in the Lake District; there most certainly are, although thanks to my HW80, fewer than there were.

Over the next few years, I became increasingly unhappy and disillusioned with my job. I was unfulfilled, under-valued and underpaid, so I went back to college to train for university. To fund my new studies I had to sell everything I had, including my beloved HW80 and all my airgun paraphernalia. It was heartbreaking and I had mixed emotions, although I still hunted at this time, by borrowing gear from friends.

After obtaining my degrees and then getting a new career, one of the first things I did was to re-engage with airgunning after my brief hiatus. The first thing was to do some research and see what had changed in the world of airguns. Beforehand, the HW80 was the weapon of choice for most serious hunters – even John Darling had one, but now there were some new kids on the block; new manufacturers, new models and some guns called Pre-Charged Pneumatics (PCPs) had really taken off. I knew nothing about them so I stayed clear of them at that time.

I did some reading, noticed a company called 'Air Arms' (AA) and read about the tuned synthetic internals in their spring guns, and some of their design innovations. I also checked out the HW80 again, which seemed to be pretty much the same and somewhat dated to me after some seven years since having sold one. Part of me said, 'If it isn't broken, don't fix it. It's just as effective as it ever was' – true, the HW80 will always be a legend in the world of hunting, but I knew that engineering and design

THE AIRGUNNER'S COMPANION

should have advanced a little over the years, so what was new out there and what were people talking about?

I wanted to ease myself back in with what I knew – spring-powered – but a more modern take on them, so I ended up going for an Air Arms TX200 Hunter Carbine (HC) with a walnut stock, and to this day, this is still my spring-powered gun of choice. A couple of years later, I bought my first PCP, an AA S410K, followed a few years later by another AA S410, but now the Classic full rifle, fitted originally with a walnut thumbhole stock.

Airguns have come a long way since those days of sitting on stone-cold ground in the family garden until the late hours on a summer evening, trying to stare at a chalked-up barrel sight in the last embers of daylight. Airguns are now more highly engineered than they have ever been, deadly precise, consistent, reliable and an absolute joy to shoot. They are a world apart from where they were when I started, but I must confess, I am still nowhere near the shot or hunter my old father was, with an ageing Webley Vulcan that kicked like a mule, a bent-haired 4x20mm scope, and shoddy pellets.

2 Why Choose an Airgun?

THE 'GOOD OLE DAYS' OF AIRGUNNING

I remember with great fondness, and probably some rose-tinted nostalgia, how I hunted with airguns when I started. All I really had was an airgun, a tin of pellets, and I merely wore dark clothes, black, green or navy, because I couldn't afford camouflage – grabbed the airgun and pellets, and off I went to the farmer's land.

On the whole, most shooting involved randomly wandering around farm buildings, fields and woods, looking for non-observant rabbits and rats. When young and full of beans, I didn't really have the patience for sitting in wait. I did it a little, but it was not my favourite pastime. Some knowledge of mating periods through the year for various quarry, their basic behaviours, and an understanding of airgun law was pretty much it.

I was hunting with airguns and enjoying the pursuit. I was sensible, safe – and certainly keen. This approach was effective in the sense that I achieved respectable bags of vermin shot on a number of forays, but by no means all. I would go shooting with some friends and there were plenty of discussions over who had the 'best' gun, all in good spirits, and that was that. For me these were the 'good ole days'. We put little thought or worry into anything and just got on with it. That's what young boys in the countryside did back then. You hunted, fished, or did both. Things were simpler and seemed to work reasonably well.

There was nothing wrong with this method, and to this day, I will often throw the guns in the car and then go for random walks over the land, just to see what might come my way by chance rather than design. It is a wonderful way to spend an autumn day or a summer evening, and I recommend this experience to anyone interested in airgunning. At times, it is best not to over-think – just do it. It is airgunning in its most basic and raw form and you will enjoy success at it, but it is not the most effective tactic and I would never describe it as providing a serious service for the farmer. We made an impact on pest species, but my experience was limited and I hunted mainly for the pot, so although it had its place in my development as an airgunner, it was not sufficient to make me a truly effective hunter. Things needed to move to another level, and over the years, I'd like to think they did.

THE PHILOSOPHY OF THE AIRGUN HUNTER

The approach and philosophy of the airgunner is very different to that of other shooting disciplines. I am not saying one is 'better' than the other, just different, and each one arguably better suited to different scenarios. Many airgunners also own shotguns, or cartridge-based rifles, and enjoy all formats. These shooters will know which tool to reach for to get a particular job done, but many stick to one format and seek to get the most out of that. Those who use only airguns under the UK legal limit (discussed later) approach shooting differently, say, than those who use only shotguns. They are different disciplines.

I know a number of people who are members of shotgun syndicates. These chaps pay landowners money to shoot over their land, and some concentrate primarily on game birds (pheasants) or wildfowl, along with some other quarry that presents itself by chance. It can be just for the sport of it, or to eat. The shotgun comes into its own league when the quarry is on the move, and some of the hunting techniques involve spooking animals to flush them out, or waiting for them to fly by the shooter who is concealed in a hide.

Sometimes, the shooter will simply stomp through the woods and see what gets spooked, or take part in organised pheasant shoots where 'beaters' will do it for them whilst the shooter looks for the birds in flight. In some cases, the pheasants are bred and fed specifically for the shoot, and could never be described as truly wild. Vermin species – grey squirrels, rabbits, and rats – will be shot, but usually only if they emerge by chance. Cartridges can be too expensive to waste on some vermin, and even more so if they are not what you are really there to bag.

None of these methods or techniques are of much use to the hunter using air rifles. Hunting with air rifles is more in line with the psychology of the sniper, relying on the concept of the planned ambush or stealth whilst stalking. The crucial idea is to work out the places giving the best cover, whilst giving access to areas that the quarry frequent. Of course, airgunners can hunt effectively when they themselves are on the move, but less so when the quarry is in motion. It is a bit like tornado hunting in the USA. You find a place where and when you know they occur, and then wait

WHY CHOOSE AN AIRGUN?

or wander around the region seeking out opportunities. If you've done your research it should pay off.

An important skill involves stalking the quarry down into range, using one's surroundings to help to conceal movement, and slowly encroach on the position of the sighted quarry. The idea is not to flush anything – quite the opposite – but if you do spook something, it can still be culled if it makes the mistake of pausing at some point, as grey squirrels and rabbits often do. Other methods require patience and lots of it. I must say that I've rarely met a shotgunner who is prepared to sit and wait, often for a few hours, to ambush grey squirrels at feeding stations. However, crucially, the different philosophies complement each other well in the overall scheme of things. Alternative formats of rifle (rimfire/centrefire) can be used for the control of vermin and game species, but the philosophy would be the same as that of the airgunner in the sense of ambushing or stalking quarry.

THE ADVANTAGES OF THE AIRGUN

There are unique advantages to using an airgun for hunting certain vermin species. An airgun can be nearly silent when fitted with a moderator, so it is entirely possible to shoot around farm buildings, near horse paddocks, poultry, sheep and pig pens without putting the farm animals under any undue stress. If you get it right, few people or animals will ever be aware of your presence. It is also relatively ecological; only one small pellet is deployed, as opposed to lots of shot as with shotguns, and this will not damage exotic tree species or foliage should you miss the intended quarry. The respective ammunition is also relatively cheap, so airguns can often be the preferred weapon of choice and offer a very serious and real alternative to other methods.

The airgun has other advantages. For example; when trying to control a rat infestation, many farmers do not want to put poison down because dogs, cats and raptors can become the unintended victims of poisoning. Shotguns might not be viable around the farm buildings due to the presence of livestock, horses, and so on, so the airgun comes into its own as a highly clinical and precise method of removing rats from the site without the need for any poison, and causing no distress to livestock. In addition, if you intend to eat your quarry – rabbit and woodpigeons – the airgun fires a single pellet, which is placed in the head of the animal, so no meat is destroyed. As a consequence, there is no need to fish the shot out of the animal when preparing for the table.

THE FRUSTRATION OF HUNTING WITH AIRGUNS

I have met many people over the years who once tried shooting with airguns, but gave up soon after. When I enquired further, the typical response was that they described becoming frustrated with airguns. They were unable to hit anything and the whole process was somewhat more demanding than they had initially assumed it would be. This reflects two important factors; firstly, for some reason that has never been clear to me, hunting with airguns seems to imply that there's a kind of 'easiness' to it, that it should be straightforward. You just put the crosshairs on the head of the critter and pull the trigger, don't you? Er, no. Secondly, hunting with airguns does require a collection of skills that might not be immediately obvious. Few people starting out realise the importance of pellet choice, of distance judgement, when and where to hold over or hold under, the best point of impact (POI), the influence of steep angles (inclination/declination) on shot placement, or that the trajectory of the pellet needs to be thought of as a curve and taken into account with the other factors outlined here. Somewhat disillusioned, many move on to shotguns or cartridge-based high-calibre rifles, and this is a shame, but understandable if you are not enjoying good results.

If we think closely about the essence of hunting with airguns, we can see why it is so demanding. On the whole, it requires sending a projectile (the pellet) smaller than the fingernail on your little finger, downrange from, say, 10–40 yards, to land within a region no bigger than the diameter of a 10-pence or 5-pence piece. The environment, the gun, and the shooter are all sources of variability that can impact on whether the outcome will be success or failure.

Some people can just pick up the airgun and have a real aptitude for it. It is intuitive to them and as their knowledge grows, their skills improve even further. Intuition and skill work in concert and result in a highly knowledgeable and able airgunner. For me, the fact that I see the clear benefits from practice when out hunting in the field and I need to call on those skills, yet on other days I can't seem to hit a barn door, is addictive. No two hunting forays are ever the same – you are constantly being tested.

WHY CHOOSE AN AIRGUN?

You need to think, so hunting with airguns is a cerebral activity. For me, the cerebral nature of hunting with airguns is a positive thing. It is an attraction to the pursuit. It takes time and effort before you will start to enjoy consistent results with an air rifle. When starting out, we all want to get into the fields and woodland as soon as possible, but time down at the practice range will be better spent as you begin with your interest. This is frustrating for many, and for those demanding instant results. Unfortunately, the skill required for hunting effectively with airguns takes time to acquire and there are no short cuts.

HUNTING WITH AIRGUNS: IT'S NOT FOR THE FAINT-HEARTED

You need to have a particular mindset in order to hunt, and to hunt with airguns in particular. It might look good on the tin, but the reality for some might be very different. If you are hunting in the UK with energy-limited airguns, then you are shooting vermin and pest species. Legal quarry would include; rats, rabbits, grey squirrels, crows, magpies, rooks, jackdaws, woodpigeons, feral pigeons, collared doves, blue jays, mink, stoats and weasels.

Hunting with airguns is all about consistency and precision in shot placement, but sometimes the shot will not go as planned and might not be as clean as intended – we are human after all. You might have pulled the shot, the wind could have blown the pellet off course, or perhaps you loaded a duff pellet. I don't want to dwell on the issue, but it would be dishonest to pretend it doesn't happen, no matter how rarely. You need to have the discipline to practise as much as you can so that such situations are as rare as they can be, and the fortitude of character to deal with it, if it does happen. On occasions, you might need to get up close and personal to your quarry. If you truly respect the quarry you shoot, you need to act swiftly and calmly should something go wrong.

Ultimately, the aim is the humane dispatching and lethal removal of vermin. If plan A is sub-optimal, you need a plan B. Cruelty is not an option. I certainly do not want to put anyone off hunting with air rifles, but I do suggest they consider the full implications of their actions before further considering whether it is for them. Although this book is about hunting with airguns, competition target shooting and hunter field target shooting, both highly enjoyable and popular, mean that you can fully enjoy the sport of airgunning without shooting any living thing, should you discover that hunting living animals is not for you.

AIRGUNS IN THE 21ST CENTURY

The tool bag of the modern airgunner is a world away from what it was when I started out. Back in the day, airguns were primarily spring-powered (springers), rarely moderated, fitted with small telescopic sights at best, although often just open barrel sights, and with poor pellet options. Lamping involved a huge lead-acid battery, which often leaked in your backpack, an old car headlight, wires, and often two people – one to hold the lamp and one to hold the rifle and shoot. Airguns were fitted with single-stage, non-adjustable and often clumsy triggers, and they kicked like a mule when fired. I remember these days with some nostalgia, but at the same time have no wish to return to them.

It is now the 21st century and I'm pleased to say that things have moved on considerably. Now, the airgunner can choose between a variety of airgun formats, such as pre-charged pneumatics (PCPs), or spring-powered units; open sights can be fitted with fibre-optics so they can be seen in the dark; the choice of pellets has never been larger and the quality of them never better; the multitude of telescopic sights available – different manufacturers, specification, and magnification – are enough to send the airgunner into a positive state of decision paralysis. A legion of sound moderators are not only available, but now seen as a necessity – certainly for PCPs – and almost all guns have high-level adjustable two-stage triggers.

Lamping is effortless. You can give your friend the night off and do it alone, with self-contained lamps the size of a cigar, with large beams and small batteries. These units just sit on top of your telescopic sight. In fact, you can give your lamp the night off and use night-vision. Laser rangefinders help with assessing distance; shooting sticks or bipods help with stability; and various customisations on stocks and gun actions add a whole new dimension to the airgunning experience. There are now even many different forms of camouflage patterns, which seem to have turned this aspect into a science, as well as providing almost full wind- and waterproofing.

Things have certainly moved on, and hunting with air rifles is a serious business. These advancements can have the capacity to make you more effective as a hunter,

WHY CHOOSE AN AIRGUN?

providing you do your bit. No amount of electronic wizardry or exotic materials will make you an effective shot without constant practice, and none of these trinkets give you fieldcraft skills. The phrase, 'all the gear and no idea' leaps to mind here. The technology of airgunning has changed, but the skills required for being an effective hunter remain pretty much the same as they always have, and these skills take time to accrue and maintain.

AIRGUNS: MYTHS AND MISCONCEPTIONS

There are a number of myths and misconceptions surrounding airguns and their effectiveness. Some of these are held by the non-shooting general public, but I have also encountered a few shooters who should know better. Nonetheless, a non-extensive list of some of the most popular misconceptions and myths are provided below. Please note, throughout this book and below, unless otherwise stated I am referring to legal non-Fire Arms Certificate (non-FAC) air rifles.

AIRGUNS ARE NOT SUITABLE FOR HUNTING

Clearly, this is not true. Airguns are not only suitable for hunting, but as we will see, they can also be the preferred weapon of choice over shotguns and cartridge-based rifles in certain circumstances. I think this myth comes from the misconception over the word 'air' (implying 'soft') and the fact that many people often use them simply for plinking in the garden, which invokes the notion that they are toys and not firearms, in the minds of some.

Modern precision airguns are very suitable for the effective hunting of vermin species. It is estimated that only 4 foot-pounds (4 ft.lbs.) of energy is required to dispatch a rabbit humanely, providing the pellet is put in the right place. A .22 calibre airgun producing 11.5 ft.lbs. of energy at the muzzle with a 16 grain pellet will generate a pellet velocity of around 570 feet-per-second – fps, a measure of velocity – as it leaves the gun. At 60 yards, it is still carrying 7.35 ft.lbs. of energy – which is 64% of the initial muzzle energy – and will be travelling at 465fps – 70% of the initial velocity – at this distance. Therefore, it is still carrying almost double the parameters it requires to dispatch vermin species humanely at this distance. The mathematics of airguns shows then that they carry the energy to dispatch vermin

THE AIRGUNNER'S COMPANION

at 60 yards, and theoretically, beyond. However, it is unlikely many of we mere mortals are anywhere near consistent enough at that distance and why conscientious responsible hunters never take on shots at those extended distances. This means that humans are the main limitation, not the gun.

A .22 CALIBRE GUN IS MORE POWERFUL THAN A .177 CALIBRE GUN

Simply, not true – both calibres are calibrated to the same limit in muzzle energy. The legal energy limit for air rifles in the UK is 12 foot pound energy (12 ft.lbs.) at the muzzle. This is equivalent to lifting a 12 pound weight 1 foot. That is the same for all calibres. This myth might come from the fact that the .22 pellet is bigger, in relation to the .177, and .22 is also a common cartridge-based calibre, so the general public get confused.

A RIFLE IS MORE POWERFUL THAN A CARBINE

This is an interesting one. In terms of muzzle energy it is not true. Both the full-length rifle and the carbine have to adhere to the same legal limits. In terms of precision in shot placement, both produce small levels of dispersion in pellet groupings, at typical hunting distances. I have never been aware of any major or significant differences between the rifle or carbine format in terms of dispersion in shot placement at these distances. Both do an excellent job. The rifle should be slightly more nose-heavy, and that might help with any muzzle flip, even for low-recoil airguns.

Personally, I believe that if there were to be a difference, then it will be most notable at the extended ranges – 50-plus yards – that target shooters encounter in competitions, likely to be more apparent for spring-powered guns, and in favour of the longer rifle barrel. However, for the hunter, in all practical senses there appears to be no significant difference between the rifle and carbine in terms of performance in the field. Target shooters might push the distance of the airgun to the extent that such differences become more apparent, if indeed they are present at all.

Note, these latter points really pertain to precision in shot placement. In terms of muzzle energy – what some people refer to as 'power' – there are no differences between a rifle or a carbine. Both adhere to the same UK legal limit.

WHY CHOOSE AN AIRGUN?   2

LAMPING IS POACHING, AND THUS ILLEGAL

Not true. Lamping certain quarry – for example rabbits – is perfectly legal, providing you have permission from the landowner to carry out such activities on their land. Therefore, lamping per se is not equivalent to poaching. Again, the general public get confused between the fact that illegal poaching probably does go on mainly at night, and by definition, so does lamping. If you are lamping rabbits with permission, it is legal. If you are lamping rabbits without permission, that is poaching, illegal, and might also be classed as armed trespass. Thus the two often get fused together in some form of fuzzy logic, fuelling the perceptions of the general public.

Providing you have permission from the landowner, lamping certain pest species – like rabbits and rats – is perfectly legal. Make sure the landowner knows when you intend to go out at night so they do not think you are a sheep rustler!

3 GETTING STARTED

KNOW THE LAW:
AIRGUNS, VERMIN, AND GENERAL LICENCES

The legal limit of muzzle-energy for a non-Fire Arms Certificate (non-FAC) air rifle is 12 ft.lbs. This can be measured by using a device called a 'chronograph'. If you do not own a chronograph your local gun shop should have one, and will only charge you a nominal fee for checking your gun's muzzle energy for you – it's a quick and simple thing to do. If an airgun is over this legal limit, and is not registered on the owner's Firearms Certificate (FAC), then the airgun is illegal and the owner is

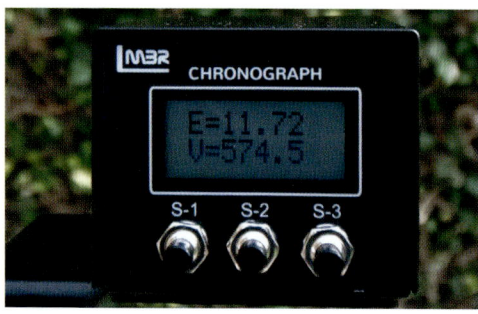

LEFT: *Determining the muzzle energy and velocity of your airgun / pellet combination is a crucial part of modern airgunning. Making sure that your airgun is always legal requires a device called a chronograph. Designs vary, but a owning a 'chronograph' helps to ensure you know your gun is legal and ascertain how it is performing.*
ABOVE: *In this example 'E' relates to muzzle energy in ft.lbs and 'V' relates to velocity in feet-per-second – fps.*

GETTING STARTED

breaking the law. The fines and penalties for owning an illegal airgun can be severe and your gun can be confiscated and destroyed, so it is therefore crucial to ensure that an air rifle is legal at all times.

The limit is not a target to aim for – pardon the pun. Most airguns work superbly at 11.5 ft.lbs. In fact, anything in the 10.5 ft.lbs to 11.5 ft.lbs. range is perfectly fine for hunting. The problem with being too close to the limit is that the muzzle energy can vary and be influenced by pellet weight and other factors – and the police can test your airgun with any pellet they choose, not necessarily the one you actually use so it is wise not to get overly close to the limit.

For storage, although airguns do not need to be kept in expensive steel gun cabinets, they do need to be secured in some way and effort must to be made to store them out of sight. They need to be secured so a minor cannot gain access to them. It is also good practice to store your ammo (pellets) in a different place to your gun. The law changes regularly and any prospective airgunners should familiarise themselves with the current law regarding the safe storage of hardware. Following best practice is a good rule of thumb, even if that means taking more precautions than the law requires. So, although it is not a requirement to lock airguns in a steel gun cabinet or equivalent, it is probably still prudent to do so. An airgun is a firearm in the eyes of the law. It is not a toy.

As previously mentioned, there are lists of species classed as pests and suitable to shoot with an air rifle, but sometimes it is important to understand context when thinking about species that can be culled humanely. For example, government agencies issue protocols referred to as 'General Licences' and they provide the legal basis for the culling of certain pest bird species. They are the law and very specific contexts can govern when it is and is not legal to shoot a given species. It is no longer the case of simply assuming that because an animal is on the 'vermin list' that you can take pot-shots at them in the garden. Things are different for some bird species, and I refer the reader to the general licences, which are reviewed every year and available on the website for the British Association for Shooting and Conservation (BASC: www.basc.org.uk). Note the licences themselves are not something you necessarily apply for. They outline the code of conduct for the legal control of certain pest bird species.

Ignorance is no defence and it is every hunter's responsibility to ensure that they are up to date with the latest airgun laws. It should also be noted that baiting certain bird species into the garden is also illegal. If you put seed out for songbirds and a woodpigeon comes flying in to feed, do not reach for the airgun. Please ensure that you adhere to the general licences at all times. Knowing the context for legal shooting is a fundamental part of being a law-abiding and responsible shooter.

ASSOCIATIONS THAT SUPPORT AIRGUNNERS

At first glance, you might not think that joining a national association is particularly important, or useful for getting started in airgunning, but in the modern world it is prudent to be a member of an association that represents the interests of airgunners, field sports, and hunting in general. There are a few associations out there to choose from and by far the biggest, and one with most political influence, is the British Association for Shooting and Conservation (BASC: https://basc.org.uk/).

As the years have passed, associations like BASC have taken on an increased prominence and relevance for all hunters. Times and attitudes have changed and for the uneducated masses, the country way of life is often seen as vulgar and abhorrent. Associations like BASC fight the corner of field sports and country life and are involved with the development of government policy, but they require your support.

I'm a proud airgun member of BASC and have written for their publication, *Shooting and Conservation*, in the past. There are a number of good reasons to be a member, but most prominent is that BASC provides you with shooting insurance. This is an excellent service. Farmers and landowners know you're serious if you are a member of BASC, an association with which they are likely to be familiar. They also have peace of mind that you are insured, and these differences just might help to seal those elusive shooting permissions. BASC also produce important updates on the ever-changing shooting laws, general licences, and what's happening around the country in field sports; clubs, societies, meetings, and so on, so it connects you to a wider community. BASC provide advice and I have found them to be very responsive and helpful to all enquiries. If you are keen about hunting, join an association that supports you. It says that you are serious about it.

LEARN ABOUT WILDLIFE SPECIES

Shooting at vermin species requires knowledge of them. It is important to know the difference between a rabbit and a hare, the rook and the raven, a red squirrel and

GETTING STARTED

a grey. Some of these are protected species, rare, endangered, and illegal to shoot; some are classed as pests or game. Out in the field, certain quarry might be far away, the light could be of poor quality, and the animal might well be partially obscured by vegetation or woodland. All these factors can come into play and influence one's perception of what you think you're looking at. If you are starting out at hunting vermin, reading up on those species, what they look like, what they sound like, their habits, breeding and feeding and so on, will prove invaluable in the field. If in doubt when looking down the telescopic sight under sub-optimal conditions, do not take the shot. If you get it wrong you might be committing an illegal act, one that will cost you financially, and could result in the confiscation of your airgun. If you are starting out, read up on the physical differences between species. Read up on the behaviour, mating patterns, eating routines, and anatomy of the animal. All this knowledge will come into play when out in the field. Never release a pellet toward a living animal unless you are 100% sure of what you are shooting at.

SPRING-POWERED AND PRE-CHARGED PNEUMATIC (PCP) AIRGUNS

Contemporary airguns come in a variety of flavours in respect to how they generate energy to propel a projectile downrange. Spring rifles, affectionately known as 'springers', are perhaps the most traditional, a tried and tested method that has differed little over decades. A high-quality, tuned spring gun is a joy to use and a very capable air weapon for hunting. They are powerful and consistent, capable of giving years of enjoyment. The big advantage of using springers is their self-contained simplicity, you just need to grab the gun, your pellets, and go hunting. The disadvantage is that they only provide a single shot at a time and they take time to re-load. They also recoil, which influences shot placement and dispersion in pellet groupings if not held correctly. There is certainly some skill required here in exploring holding techniques until you settle on one that works for you – not too firm, not too loose – in an attempt to tame the recoil.

Nevertheless, springers have been the tool of choice for many hunters over decades, including me, and in the right hands they are highly effective. I've spent countless hours out hunting with nothing but my trusted springer for company, and the wake of its effectiveness in my quarry bag on its way to my freezer. There is no doubt that shooting and hunting with a springer is airgunning in its rawest form. It is how it has been done for decades and you feel part of history doing it. Grandfather did it this way, so did father, and now you. Even though they might no longer be physically with you, in a strange way, with every trigger pull you are sharing in an experience that they once had. The apple does not fall far from the tree.

Not all change is progression, but in order to progress it is also important to welcome change and there are now some new kids on the block that give a very different, although equally valid experience. Advancements in airgun technology have led to pre-charged pneumatics, or 'PCPs' as they are known, becoming more popular and more readily available.

An under-lever spring-powered airgun (springer). A very capable weapon for effective hunting.

PCPs use a brief blast of compressed air – not gas or CO_2 – chambered from a self-contained reservoir, to propel pellets downrange. Many manufacturers make high-end models, and the hunter is certainly spoilt for choice. There are many advantages to the PCP over the springer; due to there being no mainspring/piston or movable internals of that nature, PCPs tend to be lighter than springers; they tend to be multi-shot, containing magazines that can be cycled quickly and quietly with little effort or movement. PCPs are practically recoilless, with no noticeable 'kick' to be tamed, and thus give the potential for greater consistency in shot placement and over greater distances.

The first time I ever shot a PCP, I thought it was broken! It gave me no feedback through the body at all to suggest that a pellet had actually been fired. If it were not for the hole in the paper target downrange, I would have been convinced that nothing actually left the barrel. They are also whisper quiet when fitted with a good quality moderator. Collectively, many of these factors mean that the hunter can actually take multiple shots at groups of certain species

GETTING STARTED · 3

before the rest of them fly off or run away. For the hunter, this is a not unimportant advantage. The downside with PCPs is that they need regular re-charging with air, and one needs a system for doing so. High-pressure manual pumps, like the Hills pump, or dive bottles can be used, and both are expensive and represent additional investment, but this is worth it for what these units offer the hunter.

There are some shooters out there who are as precise with a spring gun as others are with a PCP – a quality and skill I admire greatly – so it is not correct to think that PCPs are more precise than springers, but they certainly have the capacity to improve your personal performance relative to a spring gun. It is important, though, not to be lulled into a false sense of security and think they are easy to shoot and your quarry bag will be transformed overnight. This is folly. You still need to be consistent, judge your distance accurately, know your elevation, pick your spot, have a good shooting technique, breath correctly, pull the trigger in the correct manner – and so on. These issues do not disappear just because you are now using a PCP. To be effective at distance still requires considerable skill, but the advancements in engineering from using a PCP really do come into play in the field. Put simply, a PCP airgun is a multi-shot (typically), highly consistent and near-silent killer. What's not to like?

Craggy-faced old-timers, the sort that sit in the corner of the pub with their dog, flat cap, and when legal to smoke inside, Woodbines, would turn their noses up at PCPs, whilst trying to carve out some hypothetical 'purist' high ground for springers. From behind a smoke-filled haze, after drinking real ale so thick it probably had twigs in it, they will show their disdain for you and your 'modern ways'. Gravel-voiced phrases like, 'You don't know you're born', or 'It wasn't like this in my day', even 'It's all new-fangled hocus-pocus', will probably be said at some point toward you for coming out of the PCP closet[1].

Although wonderfully culturally colourful, it is complete and utter nonsense, of course. If you have a job to do then you need the tools to do it effectively. The landowner is not the slightest bit interested in whether you're shooting a customised all 'bells and whistles' PCP gun, or a 1980's spring-powered pea-shooter. He/she wants to know if the rabbits are gone, if the pigeons have been dealt with, that you've made inroads into the rats near the pig shed, that the grey squirrels have gone so that

---

1 There are still many pubs in Western Lakeland where this sort of character is still thriving – and it's a real joy to spend many an evening with them when the tales of how many rabbits they once shot in a single night grow with every pint you buy them. Oh, and be under no illusion, you're paying and the pleasure is all yours.

3 THE AIRGUNNER'S COMPANION

A recoilless, bolt-action 10-shot carbine (shorter barrel) PCP air rifle. A multi-shot, near-silent tool, ideally suited to all hunting situations.

the reds can return. Tales of the old days have no bearing on getting these jobs done, although they will put a smile on your face when thinking about them out and about in the field. Shoot what works for you with pride and enjoy it, but remember some shooting gigs require results which should always take precedent over any romantic ideals of olden times. A serious vermin problem requires a serious hunting solution.

BUYING AN AIRGUN FOR HUNTING

Which airguns are most suitable for hunting? This is a common question. Hunting with airguns involves the humane dispatching of vermin species, so the hunter needs to consider carefully. In essence, all we really want to know is whether or not a given gun can do the job. This is a good sign because it shows we want peace of mind that our tools are more than suitable. Of course, the rest is up to us to be able to get the best out of the airgun, but knowing our chosen rifles are more than capable gives us confidence in our set-up.

GETTING STARTED

We must all respect the animals that require controlling, so we need to ensure, as much as we can, that our set-ups are capable of doing the job humanely. Most of us are on a budget, but I urge caution here. Some makes of air rifles are simply not suitable for hunting. These guns might well be budget-end units, but it shows. They are not consistent, they are not precise, and are rarely fully powered. They are poorly made and give little enjoyment in shooting due to poor engineering and poor consistency. They will let you down. Avoid these at all costs and never use them for hunting.

There is an old saying, and not just in airgunning – 'buy cheap, buy twice'. An airgun is a tool; it has a job to do, it needs to be able to do that job well, do it consistently, and this quality is something we all have to pay for. There are no shortcuts and no ways to bypass this stark reality. Buying second-hand could lead to some absolute bargains, but the gamble is greater and you might need to budget for a full service or tune up, which adds additional cost.

My advice, if you've got £250 to spend, is to sit tight and save more – that amount is insufficient to buy a new, quality airgun combination suitable for hunting.

Spring-powered and pre-charged pneumatic units are perfectly suitable for hunting – as are gas-ram systems which in terms of shooting experience can be thought of as similar to springers. Assuming we are looking for a brand new gun, as a rough guide a high-quality spring gun would cost between £300–£550. This would cover excellent units from the range of Wiehrauch (HW) and Air Arms (AAs) – two companies that arguably make the finest spring guns around today. Break-barrels and under-levers are both perfectly suited for the demands of the hunter and the price range outlined above would procure models like the HW95, HW97, HW99, HW77, HW80, AA Pro Sport, AA TX200, and the AA TX200HC – all fine guns, more than capable of serious vermin control.

Along with being well suited for hunting, spring guns have the major advantage that once fitted with a telescopic sight, you are ready to hunt and there are no major additional expenses – at least as far as the gun itself is concerned. Just a tin of pellets and you're good to go, assuming you've put your practice in and are consistent with the gun in question. For PCPs the price range might be wider, and the base level probably higher. Again, a rough estimate of £500–£1000 would cover most suitable units in various specifications. Luckily, the same manufacturers as those mentioned above also happen to make some of the higher quality PCPs (HW/AAs). This price range would cover the cost of an HW100, HW110, AA S410, AA S510, AA S400, in many of their variations, and perhaps some nice woodwork as well. These are the sorts of manufacturers that the majority of contemporary hunters are using and this is not a coincidence. Of course, this is not an extensive list, and there are many other excellent manufacturers, but the ones mentioned above are the main 'off the shelf' contenders used by serious hunters, and with good reason.

These manufacturers make units of high quality, which are highly consistent, full-powered, and can be tuned into hunting rifles par excellence. Note also that these prices are for the gun alone – you still need to budget for a telescopic sight (say £160–£380), gun bag (£35), tin of pellets (£12), and possibly slings and swivels for a strap if it's a heavy springer (£30), just to get up and running. In addition, if you are buying a PCP you need to consider a method of charging the air cylinder. You can purchase a special pump for around £170, or a dive bottle – prices vary widely dependent on many factors.

If it is your first gun, or the first one in a long while, stick to known brands and keep things simple – there is no need for any major frills at this stage – then build from this solid foundation. Even if the air rifle is new, make sure the muzzle energy is below the legal limit via a chronograph. A reputable gun shop will be able to do this for you – although to be honest, it's good practice for airgun owners to purchase their own chronograph. It is illegal for a gun shop to sell you a gun that is over the legal limit, although mistakes can happen, but once you own it and you cross the path of the law some weeks/months later, you are the one in charge of an illegal gun. After having put a couple of hundred pellets through it, check its muzzle energy again. The muzzle energy can creep up once all the moving parts inside have had the chance to bed-in a little.

There are a few sub-decisions to consider before opting to buy an air rifle for hunting. One issue is which calibre to choose, and this is discussed in a separate section later because it requires some consideration. Other issues include whether to go for a rifle or a carbine, and single-shot or multi-shot.

A carbine is a gun with a shorter barrel length, often denoted by manufacturers with the letter 'K' on the end of the model number. Carbines have a number of appealing advantages for the hunter; the shorter barrel means they are easier to handle and less likely to get tangled up in foliage, or clip an obstruction in the woodlands, around the farm, or in the hide, and the carbine is more compact and easier to handle in confined spaces.

Springers (and gas-rams for that matter) are typically single-shot, and PCPs can be offered in single- and multi-shot variants. Multi-shots tend to be fed by some form of magazine which indexes the shots via a bolt or sidelever action. If considering a PCP for hunting I would recommend getting a multi-shot version because there is a big advantage to being able to cycle shots quickly and quietly in the field, with little movement or fuss. They are also just more convenient. I've taken multiple rabbits and grey squirrels within seconds of each other on many occasions with a multi-shot PCP, and this would not have been possible with a single-shot air rifle.

Choosing an exact model of airgun is a very personal thing. The way it looks and visual aesthetics can be important, as well as its build quality – it is a very personal choice. However, there is another issue rarely talked about in shooting circles which is very important – that of embodiment. Scientists know all about the concept of embodiment and how significant it is in many domains, including sport. Embodiment is related to your perception of what counts as 'part of your body' and being an aware, thinking agent inside and in charge of a physical body. Anyone who has operated a bucket digger arm will, to some degree, embody their own frame of reference to that of the device in order to use it successfully. This is the process of embodiment.

Now, in relation to airgunning, this is very much a personal thing based in part on the shooter's physical structure, natural postural biases and specific manner in shouldering the gun. Ultimately, the airgun needs to feel natural when shouldered. It needs to feel like it is part of, or an extension of, your body, somewhat akin to a longer arm. The more that this is the case, then the more 'embodied' the gun will become, and the more likely you will be successful with that particular make/model because it will have a very 'intuitive' feel for you. This is another reason why picking a specific air rifle is a very personal thing. I've gone along to an airgun shop with a particular model in mind that I wanted to try, and as soon as I shoulder it, I know if it's right for me and if I'm going to get on with it. No matter how much you have set your mind on a particular unit, or how pretty it is, if it doesn't feel right in the shoulder, the degree of embodiment will be reduced and you will always be swimming upstream against the impact of reduced embodiment when trying to get on and use it.

Factors that improve or detract from the degree of embodiment can include the rake angle on the pistol grip of the stock and the distance between the butt of the stock and trigger blade. If the rake is too steep or shallow, this can cause the shooter to contort their grip, distort their shouldering, and impact on trigger technique. Similarly, the distance from the butt of the rifle to the trigger blade can also induce other bodily contortions – stretching and contracting – in an attempt to shoulder the rifle. Studying photographs or design plans of rifles is pointless; the only way to know if the dimensions of the rifle suit your body is to pick one up and shoulder it.

Another good example of this issue relates to thumbhole stocks. Some shooters simply cannot get on with them and don't like them at all. Others, including me, find them extremely comfortable and intuitive.

Finally, it's important to bear in mind that there's a chance your airgun is better than you are. Please do not take this personally because it applies to all of us. If I strap my gun into a bench rest and explore its consistency at various distances, it out-performs me shooting from a stable sitting position every time. This should leave you in no doubt that your chosen unit is more than up to the job. The real question now is, are you?

The walnut thumbhole stock on my AA S410 Classic. Note also the adjusted butt-plate. For me, my physical body and how I shoulder and embody an airgun, a thumbhole stock is incredibly comfortable and due to its improved ergonomics, can elevate my consistency in the field for certain types of shots and hunting (i.e., ambushing). This won't be the case for everyone, but if in doubt, give one a try. Don't forget to explore adjusting the butt-plate for full effect.

WHICH CALIBRE FOR HUNTING?

When I started with airguns there was a simple rule: You shoot .177 for targets and .22 for hunting. Calibre choices are a contentious issue that can lead to heated debate within some quarters of the airgun community. It's a 'handbags at dawn' issue for many shooters and I've never really understood why. If you put the pellet in the right place, the quarry will be humanely and instantly culled, irrespective of calibre. Although there are a host of different calibres available (.177, .20, .22, .25), by far the two most popular are the .177 and the .22 and I will restrict this discussion to these variants. There are positives and negatives with any calibre, but ultimately it really boils down to personal choice.

It is important to be clear upfront about this issue; the .177 and .22 make excellent hunting calibres, both are deadly across typical hunting distances, and out to 40 yards I've never been convinced of any real difference in performance between them. Ideally, a hunter wants a pellet that travels as fast as it can and to hit as hard as it can. However, the issue is often cast that the .177 pellet travels faster, but the .22 pellet hits harder. True – but these are relative differences. To my mind, the .22 can travel more than fast enough, and the .177 can hit more than hard enough, irrespective of any relative differences[2]. In other words, these limitations are not sufficient to render either calibre useless for hunting. The real question is not, 'Which is the best calibre?', but 'What's the best way of getting the most out of a given calibre?' There are some noteworthy differences that impact on how to get the best out of the calibres.

Personally, I prefer the .22 calibre coupled to a medium-weight pellet (16 grain) for all my hunting. It simply hits hard and dumps its energy into the quarry. My opinion is based on over 35 years of shooting with airguns, and how soundly I can drop the animal in question.

The calibre of choice for competition target shooters is the .177. This smaller calibre sends a lighter pellet much faster downrange. The faster-travelling pellet means gravity has less time to exert its effect and so one observes a flatter trajectory, although it would be foolish to think distance is not important for this calibre – it most certainly is. The trajectory of the .177 is curved – no pellet can beat gravity – but markedly less so than the larger calibres. These observations have also led to

---

[2] A situation that can be improved even further with correct pellet choice for both calibres.

the perception that the .177 might make a superior hunting calibre as well. Strong advocates of the .177 also talk about the greater penetration that a .177 can achieve, where in many cases the pellet goes straight though the skull/brain and out the other side, and about the .22 calibre being 'too loopy' or the trajectory curve being too pronounced. All these arguments are vastly over-played and such 'shooters' should know better.

The main advantage of the larger .22 calibre is that it hits harder (note – paper targets do not have a pulse!) and so is potentially capable of transferring more of its energy into the quarry. Due to the more pronounced trajectory, hunters certainly need to be more aware of their distances with the larger calibre, but in all honesty, this is a skill all hunters should have, irrespective of calibre. To my mind, it is a crucial part of fieldcraft and not that difficult to learn.

My main guidance would be not to worry about either calibre being capable of doing the job. These days they are well suited to hunting vermin species, and the only job you need to do is see which one you get on with more. However, the shooter will need to do their research in terms of pellet choices – discussed later – to capitalise on the merits of any calibre. For the .22 calibre the main issue is balancing its merits with a pellet that does not give a trajectory that is too loopy. For the .177 calibre the main issue is researching a pellet that can combat its tendency to over-penetrate where the pellet can go straight through the quarry.

Ideally, you want the pellet to dump all its energy into the animal. If it over-penetrates, that means it's still carrying energy beyond the animal, which is not optimal or efficient. This is also a very real problem when shooting around farm buildings, where pellets might continue on their journey toward buildings and other unintended locations, having gone straight through the animal.

In addition, if you shoot .22 do not use a pellet that is overly heavy because this will produce a trajectory that is too curved to be bearable at longer distances, and the pellet might travel too slowly to enjoy stability along its path, and hence detract from its overall performance. Both calibres are closely matched in terms of dispersion in pellet groups over typical hunting distances, providing you do your part. Get an airgun in any calibre, seek to optimise its attributes as much as you can and enjoy the sport. My freezer tells me the .22 works and that this calibre is best for me, but I know plenty of colleagues who have the same opinion about the .177. What more is there to say?

GETTING STARTED

ESTABLISHING THE SWEET SPOT (PCPS)

All PCPs work on the same basic principle of being fitted with some form of air cylinder, from which a small charge of air is supplied to power each pellet. Although manufacturers might state a maximum and minimum air pressure giving a certain number of shots before a recharge is required, the reality is slightly different. All PCPs have what is known as a 'power curve', and as part of this, a 'sweet spot' where we get the most consistent shots with the least variability in feet-per-second (fps: velocity), thus providing a high level of consistency.

For example, Air Arms state that the S410 can be charged up to 190 bar and run until about 90–100 bar. However, the sweet spots on my guns typically range from 170 bar to 100 bar. If I fill the cylinder to 190 bar, the first few shots are under-powered and more variable. If I fill to 170 bar, then the muzzle energy is maximal and the variability low all the way down to around 100 bar. This is the sweet spot and exactly where I want to be when in the field hunting. Some airgun models are notorious for having pronounced power curves, leading to very few shots of maximum power and a large variation in fps across shots. Other models fare much better, but it is always important to establish the sweet spot. Any owner of a PCP needs to know its sweet spot to get the best performance out of the gun.

There are a number of ways one can establish the sweet spot on their PCP. The most precise way is to use a chronograph and measure the output of every shot over the entire shot string. To do this, make a note of every fps reading, per shot, from a full fill. Enter these data into a spreadsheet on computer and draw a graph. Note the point of maximal power, and then explore how many shots over the string are within a given percentage, say 1.5%, or a given variation, say 10 fps of the peak shot(s). You can then balance the degree of variability with the number of shots. For example, you might have 40 shots with 4fps variability, but 60 shots at 8fps variability, and 90 shots with 30fps variability. Ideally, you would note the highest pressure point at which the power curve started (i.e., 170 bar) and that is what you would now fill to.

In addition, you would try to ensure that you do not shoot below the point when the curve really started to drop off (i.e., 100 bar). This helps to ensure that all your shots are not only full power, but also have a high degree of shot-by-shot consistency – basically, flattening the curve as much as possible.

Although there is nothing wrong with wanting high precision in one's rifle, many in the airgun community obsess over sweet spots. For instance, in the above example, are you more seduced by sticking to the idea of a sweet spot of say 40 shots, with 4fps variability across the shot string/sweet spot, or 60 shots with 8fps variability? Is this difference really noticeable in terms of downrange precision? What is the minimum variation at which differences actually become noticeable in shooting? Knowing these fps numbers is important, but knowing how they transfer into practical differences in the field is the crucial point. I would say that some of these particular differences are far too minor to worry about. To my mind, 8fps total variability across 60 shots is absolutely excellent, and highly respectable. I'd take that as the sweet spot from this example given above. Put simply, of course we want as many shots as possible and the variability to be as low as possible, but there is a point at which such additional gains in the mathematics of the gun, will not translate into noticeable differences in actually shooting it and so become redundant.

There is another method for establishing a sweet spot, which just requires targets, distance and different cylinder fills. Fill your gun to around 150 bar, which in most

Two targets from a session establishing the sweet spot using targets rather than a chronograph.

ABOVE LEFT: *The lower four holes were the first few shots. They then slowly climbed up the target and then stopped in the pre-zeroed region (bullseye level), establishing the point of the start of the sweet spot. Across a series of other targets the centre-mass landing points stayed in the zero region.*

ABOVE RIGHT: *The end of the sweet spot. The initial shots were in the bullseye region and then started to fall, with the lowest hole representing the last shot taken, and clearly representing the end of the sweet spot.*

GETTING STARTED

cases will represent a mid-point in the sweet spot. Set a target out to around 15 yards and zero the gun at this distance. Now move the target out to your preferred zero distance – for me, that's around 28 yards – and fill the gun to its recommended maximum fill. Now aim at the bullseye and start shooting at the target, keeping a note of the number of shots you are making.

Your first few shots should fall low on the target. Do not alter your zero or your aim points. Keep shooting at the bullseye even though you're missing it. After a few shots you will see the holes in the target starting to creep up toward the bullseye. Note the point – number of shots/gun pressure – at which these holes in the target level off, stop climbing, and go no higher. This is the start of your sweet spot.

Keep shooting; the pellets should be consistent for a few tens of shots before falling again. Note the point when they start to fall – again, number of shots/pressure in the gun. This represents the end of the sweet spot. You have now established the sweet spot. Fill only up to the pressure when the pellets first reached the high point on the target, and shoot only down to the pressure when they started to drop on the target. Now re-zero your gun at your preferred distance, within the sweet spot and you're good to go.

CUSTOM AND TUNED AIR RIFLES

In the UK, we are lucky in that there are a number of skilled people who can seriously improve how efficiently an airgun works. They provide a special service; they can tune your gun, customise it, or sell you one that's been made in line with tried and tested improvements developed over the years and known to work. I'm old enough to remember the legendary Venom Custom tuning shop who did amazing things with spring-powered models like the HW77 and HW80 – the famous Lazerglide tune. As a schoolboy enthused with a passion for hunting with airguns I had a fantasy of owning a Venom-tuned HW80 with a Tyrolean custom walnut stock. Sadly, I never owned one, and even sadder, Venom is no longer in operation, but other companies now exist that seek to provide a similar service, and Sandwell Field Sports in Birmingham springs to mind as a company for the airgunner to visit. Their tuned springers are the stuff of legend and are being enjoyed by many airgunners around the UK.

There are several tweaks that can be explored on spring and PCP airguns. These can be for purely aesthetic reasons, i.e., fitting a walnut custom stock – although this also improves balance – or they might have a more serious purpose such as improving muzzle energy, and consistency. Known by the community as 'fettling', such tune-ups involve all sorts of processes. It is important to remain aware of the fact that no amount of fettling should take your gun over the legal limit of muzzle energy, so one is only seeking to increase muzzle energy if the airgun was originally seriously low on muzzle energy in the first place. Fettling really makes things smoother, slicker, more efficient, more consistent, and simply sweeter to shoot.

For spring-powered airguns there are two main routes people take when thinking of improving their gun. One is to buy what is known as a 'drop in' kit which you fit yourself. These kits vary, but on the whole contain specific combinations of internal parts – springs, guides, seals, etc – which, as the name suggests, you simply 'drop into' your gun and adjust accordingly.

The other route is to get your airgun fully tuned by a professional. Different tuners might use different approaches and tweaks to airgun models, but this approach is one that is typically based on years of experience of what works and what does not. Existing parts might well be re-worked, re-engineered, machined or lathed, or replaced completely for bespoke components that have been found to be superior to production-level parts from the manufacturer. Internals might also be polished and lubricated, spring guides and 'top hats' fitted, adjusting spacers, swapping out trigger units, short-stroking, barrel adjustments, and so on. Top tuners are often devoted airgunners themselves, or work very closely with the broader community and be sensitive to the specific needs of hunters and target shooters. Tuners do not just think of the process in terms of a single part, like fitting a better mainspring. This is too simplistic. The approach is far more elegant, when all the parts, working together and in concert, are considered as part of the bigger picture of improving airgun efficiency. This understanding can only come from skilled people who appreciate the role of every single component, and how changing any particular part might impact on the operation of the whole airgun. It should be clear from the above discussions that fitting drop-in kits and getting a proper tune-up are not the same thing, but both offer different routes to improved efficiency in the operation of the airgun.

Despite not having traditional moving parts, springs, pistons and so on, there is still a lot that can lift the performance of an off-the-shelf PCP. Again, internals can be polished and lubricated (striker rails, hammers), seals replaced, ports cleaned, spacers added, and so on. The energy curve can be extended and moved up or down

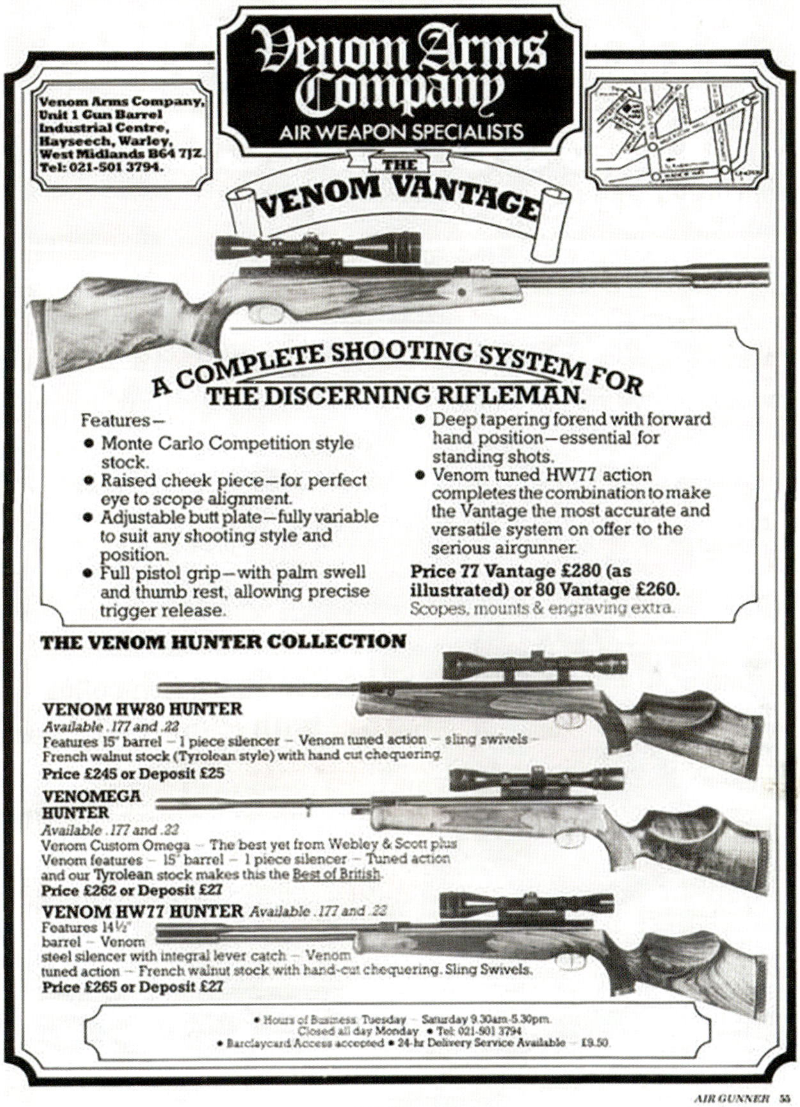

GETTING STARTED 3

Childhood dreams. An example of the Venom Custom shop advertisement from the 1980s. These were, without doubt, revered as the finest spring-powered airguns available. Custom walnut Tyrolean stocks made them look unique, as well as making them amazing to shoot. To many, these represented the pinnacle of airgun engineering from that time period and have legendary status among spring-powered enthusiasts.

THE AIRGUNNER'S COMPANION

the range of usable air pressure, and there can be improved shot-to-shot consistency. Fettling can involve minor tweaks or major overhauls. Always seeking improved precision in engineering to provide the ultimate shooting experience is an important part of modern airgunning. If done properly, a tune-up can only help to improve how your gun works and this should contribute to increased confidence in the field, increased enjoyment, and increased efficacy.

You might be tempted to fettle your airgun yourself – airguns are, after all, relatively simple, but I would advise caution here. Personally, I never touch any of my airguns and always take them to a qualified RFD (Registered Firearms Dealer) or established tuner for servicing or tuning. Seek out people based on recommendation and do not just hand your pride and joy over to a guy who reckons he 'knows a thing or two from the Internet' or some random bloke from down the pub. I'm a great believer in supporting local gun shops and RFDs. If the skills of the airgun tuner are to remain accessible to all of us, we need to support the good ones, so that they can continue to provide an excellent service to the community.

I often find some hunters are forever fiddling with their guns in an almost obsessive manner, constantly seeking more of an 'edge' that they hope will transform their hunting. To my mind, a lot of this can be simply chasing rainbows. Time is better spent working on our fieldcraft. There may be some correlation between those who constantly fiddle and those who need to fiddle even more because of their own initial fiddling! I'd much rather be out shooting with a unit that's been looked after by top professional people I trust, and simply treat the guns to what's needed as and when it's needed. In those periods between services and tune-ups, I just hunt, and concentrate on developing my skills and the job that needs doing. Once your airgun is singing sweetly, leave it well alone and just shoot with it!

THE BEST PELLETS FOR HUNTING

In the old days, there were few pellets to choose from and they were often very dirty and not well made. Luckily, things have changed and there has been something of a revolution in pellet choice and quality over the years. Newcomers to shooting often want to know which pellet is the best for hunting, and the answer is simple, but then requires some discussion. The best pellet is the one that gives the smallest degree

GETTING STARTED

of dispersion in shot placement at typical hunting distances[3]. Dispersion refers to the spatial distribution or spread of the individual pellet landing points, related to your intended aim, and ideally, you want a pellet with high consistency and low dispersion – leading to tighter groups. Pellets need to be consistent across a variety of conditions and over a host of ranges – say 15–40 yards for hunting. Basically, tight groups rule.

As discussed previously, airguns are all about precision in shot placement. Put the pellet where it needs to be and its 'game over' for the quarry, so you need a high-class pellet that can transfer all that quality from your high-end airgun into downrange clinical precision in shot placement, and to do so consistently. Your only connection to the quarry you are shooting is through the pellet you send. It is utterly pointless to spend £800 on a rifle or scope only to put poor quality pellets through it. Having acknowledged this, it is also worthwhile thinking about some of the important factors that enable a pellet to perform at a level suitable for the humane dispatch of vermin species. Pellets differ tremendously in shape, length, weight, head size and lead composition. Some pellets have a pointed head, some a rounded head; some are hollow-points, some have a harder lead composition and some are softer. Pellets can show different preferences for barrels – some can give exquisite performance and others make it hard to hit a barn door. There are some general rules of thumb for working out which are likely to give you the best performance in the field.

Contrary to intuition, pointed–pellets are of little use for serious hunting. This is due to the fact that they are not very stable in flight and so do not fly as efficiently as other styles. To be effective, airgun pellets need to maintain the spin and flight path imparted to them from the rifle barrel. For optimal results, the spin needs to rotate around a clear central axis producing a stable rotation. Pointed pellets rarely have their points directly on the central axis of the pellet and thus are prone to wobble when spinning, and this will impact on their trajectory downrange, leading to greater dispersion in pellet groupings. If the pellet does not go where it is intended, it is useless for hunting. For these reasons, avoid pointed pellets for hunting at distance. There are also many variants of hollow-point designs. These might hit harder than other designs, but are not as consistent at increased distances, so they make an ideal rat pellet out to 20 yards, but are of little use much beyond that.

---

3   When evaluating a pellet for its suitability, it is important to explore its performance at typical zero/hunting distances. Poorer pellets will soon be revealed under these more challenging conditions.

Round-headed, domed pellets – referred to as 'diabolo' pellets – are by far the best all-rounder for hunting, because they are the most stable in flight and this leads invariably to the highest level of consistency and smallest dispersion. Round-headed pellets fly more efficiently, fly straighter, with less wobble relative to pointed pellets, and they give the tightest dispersion, over distance, relative to all other designs. As noted elsewhere in this book, when hunting live quarry consistency is king, therefore the pellets that group best are the ones that will give best results in the field.

Having decided on the most suitable shape, the next thing to think about is the ballistic coefficient (BC). The BC of a pellet is a measure of how efficiently it resists air drag and retains velocity as it travels downrange. The larger the coefficient of the pellet, the lower the loss in velocity, so higher numbers are what we want. According to the computer programme, Chairgun (Hawke Optics), AA Field Diabolos and JSB Exact Jumbos have the highest BC of any pellet in their class (0.03 for an approximate 16 grain pellet in .22) making these prime contenders as the best pellet. If these pellets like your barrel and group well, then you would be hard pushed to find a better pellet for hunting.

Another factor is weight, but the right weight of a pellet for your airgun will depend on the calibre you are shooting. Weight is most often talked about in terms of 'grains'. Some shooters want a lighter pellet because they fly faster and give a flatter trajectory; others want heavier pellets based on the idea that heavier pellets will hit harder. Both concerns are well-founded, but there are some general mitigating factors that should be considered. For example, for users of the .22 calibre if this idea is taken too far, heavy pellets can be problematic for an airgun limited in muzzle energy. In terms of heavy pellets in a .22 PCP, I have tried both AA Diabolo Field Plus Heavy (18 grain), and H&N Baracuda Hunter Extreme (19 grain) as heavy-grain alternatives. The AAs are similar to the standard AA Diabolos, based on the round-head style, only heavier. The Baracudas have a cross-head design, and are thought of as akin to hollow-points. Both pellets are extremely well made and very clean in the tin.

The results of my own informal tests tell me that both pellets are far too heavy, in .22, to be useful beyond 25–28 yards. They might hit hard, but their range is limited for a sub-12 ft.lbs., .22 calibre airgun. The slow movement means gravity has more time to pull the pellet down and thus the trajectory becomes very loopy. Reduced speed could also impact on the pellet's stability in flight. In my opinion, these pellets are really aimed at the FAC market when we think of them for the .22 calibre, and in that context they will be absolutely devastating.

However, the equivalent pellets can be excellent in the faster flying .177 calibre, which travel much faster, and this extra speed can make more effective use of the Baracuda/AA heavier design.

As a very general rule then for sub-12ft.lbs. PCP airguns, for the .22 calibre I would recommend a hunting pellet of around 15–16 grains (AA Diabolos/JSB Jumbo Exacts, etc) – going heavier will just make the trajectory very loopy at distance.

For the .177 calibre, and again in PCP format, a general rule for hunting would be to avoid pellet choices that promote over-penetration as this is not efficient. This may take some experimentation on your part. If you have a barrel that likes lots of different pellets then you have room to explore these factors. If your barrel is pellet fussy – then stick with the one that gives tight groups as that is the primary factor that should guide your decision. So, our decisions on pellet choice are always a trade-off between all these factors and we need to make an 'on balance' assessment of what is best for us. This requires research on your part so it's well worth putting in the time and effort.

There is a general view that a lighter pellet works better than a heavier one, both in .177 and .22, in spring-powered airguns. PCPs are said to prefer heavier pellets. To be honest, I've never really been aware of any major differences and for many years have shot a 16g pellet out of a spring-powered gun with no noticeable issues. Ultimately, it is down to the shooter to do their research and work out which pellets like your barrel and lead to sweeter shooting.

A further decision is head size. Many brands make the same pellet, but with slightly different head sizes. The issue of head size is controversial in the community. Some airgunners do not think that such small differences in head size can be achieved with the modern methods of pellet production, or at the very least, are not consistently packaged in the factory – meaning your tin of pellets might actually contain different head sizes. Others swear by the fact that they have observed differences in the zero of their airgun – suggesting that the pellets are fitting the barrel and using the air differently.

One experiment I ran was to zero my gun at 27–28 yards with AA Field Diabolos of a 5.51mm sizing, and then switch to 5.52mm, and there was absolutely no difference in terms of the zero of the gun. The pellets landed in exactly the same place on the target. Therefore, for my airguns and pellet choices, I know such claimed differences in head size appear to have no discernible influence on downrange groupings. This might not be the case in all circumstances and combinations.

I have heard some people say that you can pick pellets based on the variation in fps as measured by a chronograph at the muzzle. I disagree. It is entirely possible that pellets giving little muzzle variation could, in theory, produce poor grouping downrange. Conversely, pellets giving more variation at the muzzle might indeed group better downrange. The reasons for this are complicated, but put simply, some pellets can become more stable as they travel downrange, and others more unstable. Again, the simple rule is, stick to the pellet giving the tightest groups at your zero distance downrange because these are most likely to be the optimal pellet for your barrel.

The high-end target shooters will often weigh and size every pellet for competitions, but for me, life is too short. I do wash and lube them and throw away deformed pellets because I don't want to be fiddling in the field with duff pellets so I always do this at home before shooting. Lubricating pellets will not increase muzzle energy and it is questionable that it has any major effect, but it does help to keep the pellet and barrel clean.

One effective way to clean and lubricate pellets is to half fill a container with warm water and a light splash of washing-up liquid. Gently place your pellets into a sieve and lower this into the soapy water. Carefully run your fingers through the pellets and move them around for a short period in the water. Note how the soapy water becomes very dirty. Now lift the sieve, drain the pellets of soap suds, and rinse under the tap. Once done, place the pellets onto a paper towel and lightly dab dry. Then take a palm bellows with a nozzle – you can buy these from camera/photography shops – and blow off the excess water from the pellets. The compressed air also helps to remove the last of the dirt. Once done, add pellets to a clear plastic bag and add a small squirt of pellet lube (I use LT1 lube). Move the pellets around within the bag to ensure that all pellets are fully coated and then, empty onto a fresh paper towel and again, use the bellows to blow off any excess lubricant. The result needs to be a clean and dry pellet. You do not want the pellet to be wet or tacky. Then pop them back in the tin or your pellet shell/holder ready for use. Make sure that you clean the tin or the pellet shell as well.

A small container for carrying your pellets in the field, and keeping them clean, is a good idea. Do not take your tins in your pockets because the noise will be unbearable and your pellets will become deformed as they shake about with every

GETTING STARTED

step. If I am shooting with PCPs, as well as a pellet holder, I will prepare around four magazines and have these loaded up and ready to swap quickly. During quiet times or when I return to the car, I'll top up any empty magazines should that be required at the time. In summary, the best pellets for hunting are round-headed diabolo pellets, which give the smallest measure of dispersion (tightest groups) at respectable distances. If you find a few brands give comparable results give further consideration to the ballistic coefficient, and weight. Remember, low dispersion rules.

Pellet preparation. Tins of pellets, a sieve, pellet lube, paper towels and a rubber bellows blower for blowing off remaining water/dirt or excessive lube. The palm bellows is better than a hairdryer because it releases a small burst of pressurised air, which helps to remove excess lubricant and any remaining dirt.

A clam-shell pellet holder and four airgun magazines prepped and ready for the field. Preparing multiple magazines means swapping them out in the field is simple and painless. It's a worthwhile tactic if you're using a multi-shot PCP for hunting.

3 THE AIRGUNNER'S COMPANION

Examples of round-headed pellets. ABOVE LEFT: *AA Field Diabolo (16g) and* ABOVE MIDDLE: *JSBs Exact Jumbos (15.9g) – both excellent, all-round hunting pellets.* ABOVE RIGHT: *AA Diabolo Field Plus Heavy (18g) which are more suited to short-distance hunting in sub-12 ft.lbs. airguns, or all shooting in FAC-rated airguns. Note both the AAs and the Jumbos have been washed and lubricated. The Plus Heavies have not been prepared.*

TELESCOPIC SIGHTS (SCOPES)

Although open-sights are fine at short distances, most serious hunters equip their airguns with telescopic sights (scopes). Scopes come in a variety of flavours, including diverse magnification, objective lens size, parallax adjustment, and with additional variation in crosshair (reticle) design. Some of these reticles are, to my mind, as cluttered as a pensioner's mantelpiece and far too busy to look through; others, arguably, are too simple. It is all down to personal choice, although I'd suggest if shooting with the .22 calibre, then compensation points (i.e., mil dots or equivalent) in the reticle are particularly useful. There are many leading manufactures who make scopes with the airgunner in mind, including; Hawke, Nikko-Stirling, Nikon, Bushnell, and MTC, as well as many others. It is really up to the individual to think about what they feel is most important, what they can live with and what they can afford. For the hunter, a rugged construction where the scope holds its zero well, provides excellent light transfer and crisp images are arguably the most important features to look for first.

A good choice would be a known brand scope, rated for airguns, recoil-proof, fog-proof, and water resistant, with a reasonable sized objective lens – 32–40mm is typical. A large objective lens helps to capture more light, but then so do better

GETTING STARTED 3

quality optics and coatings on the lenses. This is not trivial and what many hunters opt for will be a balance between cost and size. For example, the high-quality glassware could cost you well over £700 for an objective lens size of say, 40mm, and because of the quality of the glass, you probably don't need to go bigger in terms of size. However, do you have £700-plus to spend on a scope alone? Many hunters buy cheaper glassware, but bigger objective lenses as a compromise, and good-quality optics are available for around £150–£380, which is typical for a solid scope more than capable for the job. A large objective lens means you need high mounts on the gun and, of course, it will be heavier – more factors to be considered in this trade off – and sometimes such large objective lenses are unnecessary.

Extra features on scopes are fine, but only if they are important for how you shoot. For example, illuminated reticles are useful for low-light shooting in woodland – otherwise you can lose the crosshair in amongst the dark branches – but unnecessary with lamping or shooting in open fields in broad daylight hours. A large magnification range is nice in that it gives you options (i.e., x4–x12), but the chances are you will rarely move from mid-values (say x6–x10 in these examples) for general shooting and so some of these options might be excessive for sub-12 ft.lbs. airguns unless you have particular requirements in your style of shooting. Features that help are important to have. Features that do not help are expensive and redundant. Check out the scope before buying and make sure that you are happy with the reticle design, build quality and light transfer. Do not go for scopes with lots of features unless you're going to use them. If it's your first scope, there might be some trial and error before you find the perfect fit for you.

Once you have decided on a make, and possibly even an exact model, with a certain reticle design, objective lens size and zoom, there are still additional considerations to take into account. For example, many scopes have an adjustable parallax. Briefly, parallax error is an optical issue that has the potential to make you completely miss the target, even when your sights are perfectly zeroed. To experience parallax error look down a scope at a target and, once the crosshairs are positioned on it, slightly move your head left or right. If there is a large degree of parallax error then the crosshairs/reticle will be seen to move quite a bit in relation to the target. If the parallax adjustment has been calibrated for the target distance then this movement will be minimised. The movement you experience is the parallax error, an apparent perceived movement that occurs due to changes in the line of sight. This 'parallax error' effect can be reduced by an adjustable parallax on the scope, with the potential to improve consistency across a variety of distances. The idea with the adjustment here is to set it so that the picture down the scope is in crisp focus and that includes the reticle and the target, so there is minimal movement of the crosshair on the target at a set distance.

Adjustable parallax comes in two main classifications – either via an adjustable objective lens (referred to as an A/O) or a parallax adjuster on the side of the scope near the reticle adjusters. Both do the same job. Some hunters feel that parallax adjustment is just one extra thing that you do not really need in the field, prefer not to be

Modern airgun telescopic sights come with a range of features including; (i) an array of multi-coated optics, (ii) different sizes of objective lenses, (iii) adjustable eye-pieces, (iv) parallax adjustment (side-adjuster or A/O), (v) a choice of reticle designs, (vi) a large magnification range (if desired), (vii) adjustable illuminated reticles, and (viii) fog- and waterproofing, to name but a few.

GETTING STARTED

distracted by it and that it's irrelevant for hunting. I've had many scopes over the years, some with and some without a parallax adjuster, and non-adjustable scopes are absolutely fine, providing they have been manufactured with the airgunner in mind and have been corrected for airgun distances. If you have a good technique, you will still enjoy excellent performance with a fixed-parallax scope and it is possible to calibrate the parallax on fixed-parallax scopes – although this requires some knowledge about what you are doing, and it's not a thing that can be done in the field.

One final consideration which is becoming more of an issue in recent years is that of the focal plane of the scope's reticle. The most common is what is known as a 'rear' or 'second focal-plane' design. Put simply, this means that if you change the magnification of the scope image, the reticle – and its markings – never change. It always stays the same size even though the image in the scope (i.e., the target) alters with changes in magnification. The big disadvantage of second-plane scopes is that the compensation points in the reticle will only be accurate at the magnification with which you zeroed your gun. So, using examples provided elsewhere in this book, for my own combos, one compensation point down is the new zero for 40 yards – but only on x6 magnification. If you alter the magnification this is no longer true.

The other variant is a frontal, or 'first focal-plane' design. With these scopes, not only does the size of your target vary as you alter the scope's magnification, but the size of the reticle alters in sympathy with it – the big advantage is that the compensation points are always accurate, on any magnification setting. The main problem with these models is that the reticle itself, and its compensation markings, can become difficult to see on certain lower magnification settings. The vast majority of airgun scopes are second focal-plane designs and in practice these seem perfectly suitable over typical airgun hunting distances. All you have to do is make sure that if you're using a compensation point in the reticle, you are on the correct magnification for that judgement – not that hard to do in practice.

SOUND MODERATORS

Commonly referred to as 'silencers', although more accurately known as 'sound moderators', most modern airguns are fitted with such moderators to assist in the field. On a PCP, a sound moderator is a necessity for effective hunting because they are very loud without them. On a springer, a sound moderator helps a great deal, but there will always be mechanical noise from the gun itself that cannot be eliminated by a barrel-mounted moderator. Nevertheless, the phenomena known as 'barrel crack' (the loud noise from the pellet leaving the barrel) is improved by a moderator in all cases, and so there are still big improvements to be had.

There is no such thing as the 'best' moderator. Certain models might work differently on certain airguns. A good moderator does not just reduce sound, it also diffuses it. Vermin might still hear your shot, but will not be able to pinpoint where it is coming from and so will not know what to do. Many sound moderators are out there for the airgunner to explore. At the time of writing, good sound moderators include models from HW, and the Q-Tec from Air Arms, but it is an ever-changing market and new models are always emerging. I cannot think of a really good argument not to fit an airgun with a moderator, but it is important to get one that works well for the gun in question.

Some moderators are made from modern materials, like carbon-fibre, and weigh very little. Others are made out of more traditional materials which weigh a little more, but this weight can help with any form of muzzle flip, no matter how minor, and thus might help with the balance of the gun and the shooting experience it delivers. Some moderators are quite long and it's important to make sure that your airgun can still fit inside your gun bag once the moderator is fitted.

The Air Arms Q-Tec moderator ensures that my PCPs are whisper quiet. A good-quality moderator is an essential piece of kit for a modern PCP destined for the fields and woodlands.

GETTING STARTED

GETTING TO KNOW YOUR COMBINATION

Having purchased your gun, mounted your scope, and fitted your moderator, you really need to get to know how it performs. This does not involve taking it out and treating it to fine wines and Belgian chocolates, but it does involve you establishing its muzzle energy, its consistency and finding the right pellet for it, which will require some experimentation. Your gun/scope/pellet is referred to as your 'combo' and it's now time to understand how it all comes together.

You can buy pellet sample packs, which give you a small number of pellets to try from a variety of manufacturers. Get a few leading brands and experiment. The only equipment you need at this stage is a paper target set at a suitable zeroing distance. As noted previously, the best pellet is the one that gives the least dispersion (spread) in the target. Nice tight groups are the goal here. Even different guns of the same model can behave quite differently so if you are serious about hunting, you simply have to put your research in and find a pellet that likes your barrel. Once done, put a few hundred of your preferred pellets through the barrel and things will soon 'bed in', settle down, and now you can set about seriously zeroing your airgun.

Assuming you've followed the general guidance above, then your set-up or 'combo' (gun/scope/pellets) should be more than capable in all hunting scenarios. I tend to make no changes to my set-up whether I'm hunting rabbits, woodpigeon, crows, magpies, grey squirrels, or whatever. I use the same pellets and the same zeroed distance – a 27–28 yard zero – guided by pellet choice – is optimal for my PCP guns. For .177 something around 33–35 yards – and again, depending on pellet choice, is typically optimal. I try to change as little as possible and keep things as simple as possible, and this helps me to gain a really intuitive feel of my combo. The hunter who knows one set-up really well, will always outperform the hunter who has a more shallow understanding of more combos. The spirit of this idea is captured by the old saying, 'Beware the hunter who only has one gun!'

Before going any further, it is important to note that airgun pellets have what is known as a 'parabolic' trajectory. This means that you need to think of a pellet's path as being like a curve. In reality, this pattern reflects the interaction between the scope alignment, barrel position and pellet path, but relative to the crosshairs, this is how it is best to think of things – the pellet doesn't really rise relative to the central bore of the barrel. In essence. it also means you can have two zero points, one at a low distance where the pellet appears to 'rise' and cross the sight line, and the other at

3 THE AIRGUNNER'S COMPANION

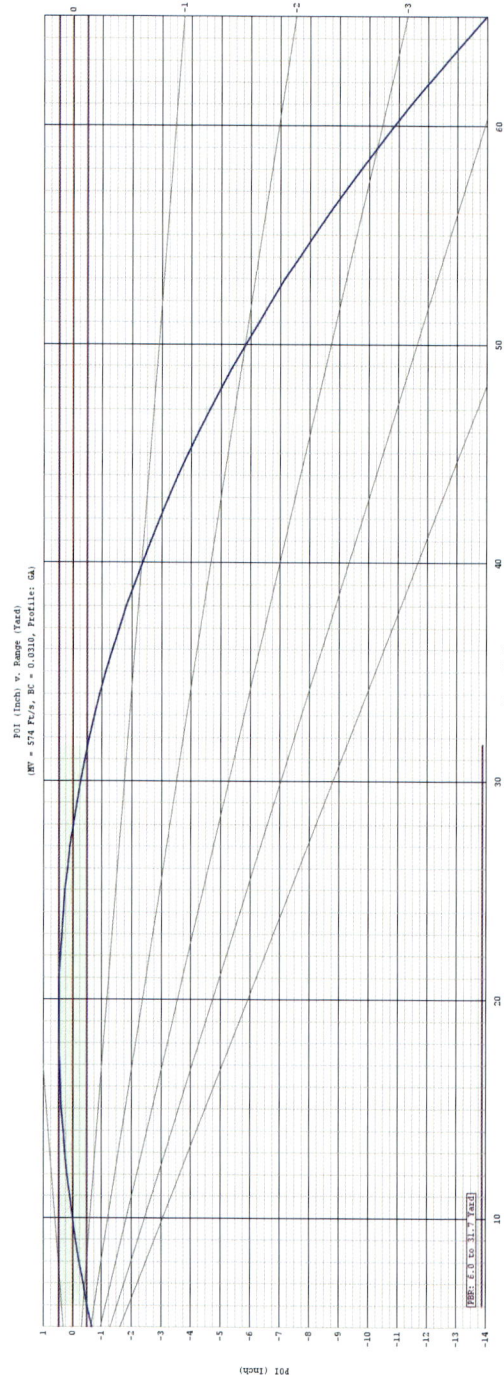

An image from the program 'Chairgun' by Hawke Optics. The blue line shows the parabolic (curved) trajectory of a .22 AA Field Diabolo pellet fired from my S410K with 11.61 ft.lbs. of muzzle energy. The middle, red horizontal line represents the crosshair line of sight in the scope. Note: the pellet actually crosses the line of sight twice, giving two zero points – one at around 10 yards and the other at 28 yards. The purple horizontal boundary lines show a 1-inch diameter range – that's 12mm above and below the crosshair – from approximately 6 –32 yards.

Note also that the radial diagonal downward lines represent mil-dot compensations for the scope. With the magnification of my Hawke scope set to around x6, the curved blue line crosses exactly at the first compensation point down for 40 yards (saying that the 1st marker is the new zero at 40 yards), and it also crosses very close at 50 yards for the second marker down – easy to remember when out in the field. Field testing these numbers is also a crucial part of this process to ensure, as much as one can, that your combo is performing how you expect it to. By appreciating this trajectory in my mind, and having confirmed them on the range, I can now be confident in the field of which aim points to use from 10– 50 yards, if I need them.

the actual zeroed distance where the pellet drops to it. In addition, the line of sight will be below the pellet at intermediate distances between the two zero points. If this all sounds too complicated, do not worry. It is simply important to appreciate and visualise a curved trajectory between you and the target downrange.

For my .22 PCPs, a zeroed distance of around 27–28 yards, gives an effective zeroed range of around 6–32 yards with the pellet having a spread of no more than 24mm (12mm above or below the exact zero point) across that range (see image above). You can explore these dimensions in computer programmes like Chairgun, which is free to download from the Hawke website.

The next step is to explore your pellet's performance at different distances and learn your compensation points in your scope. Most of my scopes are fitted with a mil-dot or mil-dot-style reticle, which is really useful for marking out compensation points with distance – and wind. Again, Chairgun tells me that at around x6 magnification on my Panorama/Airmax scopes, the first major marker down is bang on for targets at 40 yards. In other words, my pellet will have dropped a certain amount by 40 yards and to compensate I use the first large marking below the actual crosshair, as the new zero point. For me, it's really nice that for the second marking down, I'm just a smidge off for 50 yards, which is far beyond my typical personal shooting distance, but it is nice to know. So, knowing this means that I can cover a respectful and effective distance with confidence[4]. I tend to keep my scopes on around x6 magnification for general use, confirmed by range-testing to ensure that the situation above is realised with objective testing, often only altering them when scanning the wilderness or in low light.

Even if you do not have a computer program to help you, do your homework with setting targets at different distances. Keep it simple by sticking with a given magnification and learn the aim points in the reticle. This is all part of getting to know your combo. Use software like Chairgun to get you going but nothing beats proper testing. Also, do not worry too much if you need to make minor adjustments in the field, based on your testing. Not all scopes have highly accurate magnification markers and so you might have to make some fine adjustments when testing on the range. This is normal and to be expected.

---

4   You can of course choose to dial in adjustments directly on the turrets as many do with more powerful rifle units, and effectively just alter the position of the crosshair with every shot. I find this approach somewhat cumbersome and protracted in hunting scenarios with an air rifle.

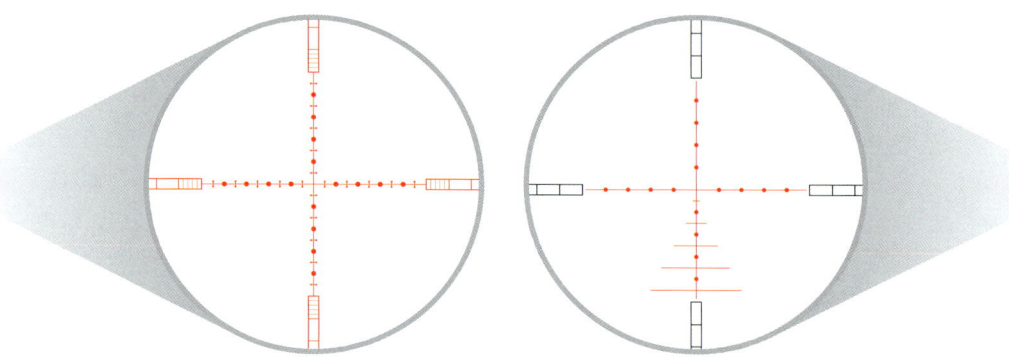

A schematic illustration of a mil-dot-style reticle (containing full and half mil dot spacing; Hawke Panorama scope on the left) and a variation of this principle (the AMX reticle, Hawke Airmax scope on the right). Aim points for adjusting for wind (horizontal line) and distance (vertical line) are clearly marked. Note, on 2nd focal plane scopes, altering the magnification on the scope will influence what the aim points correspond to in the environment. IMAGES COURTESY OF HAWKE OPTICS.

ZEROING YOUR RIFLE FOR OPTIMAL PERFORMANCE

Actually, this is a method for zeroing and practising your shooting technique because the two are dependent on each other to some degree. I should say that this method is not something to do regularly, or at the beginning of every shoot, when one might just check things quickly by shooting at the odd acorn, pebble, or leaf. This is more something to do when mounting or changing scopes, buying a new gun, after a tune-up, or any major changes you've made to a gun. Having said that it is always good to do a check-up of this nature so that you have absolute confidence in your set-up. Some might think this is overly excessive, and perhaps you could find short-cuts, but this method works for me.

You Will Need:

Airgun, scope, pellets, bench rest, targets: paper with crosshairs marked on them set at an optimal zero range, rangefinder, Hawke Chairgun computer program, or similar, and a plumb line.

GETTING STARTED 3

GENERAL APPROACH

A two-phase approach is best. The first phase is about establishing the 'mechanical zero' of the gun (via some form of supported/rest shooting). The second phase involves minor tweaks from shouldering the gun more naturally without a bench rest. Then you're good to go. The process takes time to do properly, but the results are impressive in terms of gaining a really accurate zero. What is described here is for a PCP but the principles apply to all airguns.

OTHER EQUIPMENT

Apart from the obvious gun, scope, and pellets, I'd recommend a good-quality support, like a bench rest or beanbag, and a sturdy table from which to shoot. It is important that the gun is supported at a height that does not induce body contortions in the shooter because these will impact on how you look through the scope. It needs

My S410 Classic about to undergo a zeroing session. Make sure the gun and scope are level (no cant) and the air pressure is in the sweet spot. The scope is set to a mid-magnification and the adjustable objective lens calibrated to a laser-distanced target around 28 yards (.22) or around 33–35 yards (.177) downrange. Supported shooting – a bench rest, bean bag or whatever – helps to establish the true mechanical zero as an important first stage of the process (see text).

THE AIRGUNNER'S COMPANION

to feel natural to you. You also need some decent paper targets, those with crosshairs or similar on them for you to align your scope – more on that later.

Your Scope

Make sure your scope is level and the eye-relief is correct. You can do this in a number of ways; to make sure it is level, you could use a plumb line and ensure that the vertical line in the scope is calibrated to the plumb line. Ensure that you do not canter the gun during this process. You can also do this in a bench rest.

A neat trick for assessing eye-relief on the scope is to close your eyes and shoulder the gun so it sits comfortably – now open your eyes. The whole view should be clear with no black tunnelling or blur around the edges. If not, adjust the scope forward or backward, until the whole reticle lights up, which typically gives around one to two inches of eye relief. I repeat this process a few times, until I know there is no need for any further adjustments to my head position once the gun is in my shoulder. Often ignored is an adjustable butt-plate on the stock. If you have one, explore it – it transformed things for me with my thumbhole stock in regard to excellent eye-relief and perfect shoulder position and posture. The final aim is a fast shouldering action with minimal, if any, head adjustment once the gun is in the shoulder and you are looking down the sight. You should NOT be 'hunting' for the reticle to light up fully once the gun is in the shoulder. The optimal view should simply be there with no effort.

If your scope has an adjustable parallax feature (A/O or side-wheel) then set this for the zero distance – in my case 27–28 yards – because it is easy to forget to do this. Make sure that the paper target and the reticle are both crisp and sharp. The degree of parallax error experienced should also be minimal if this has been done properly. If you struggle to make this decision, turn up the zoom magnification to set the parallax, but put it back to your typical magnification for the rest of the zero process because on some scopes, your zero can alter at vastly different magnifications. Adjust the eye-relief dial on the eyepiece if required; get everything in crisp focus and this can also thicken up the crosshairs slightly to a more desirable level.

Stock Sweet Spot

Sweet spots are not just in terms of air pressure levels. It also pertains to the ideal head position on the stock to produce a full field of view down the scope, and a comfortable

GETTING STARTED

shooting posture. The head can rotate in three dimensions – left/right, up/down, and the degree of roll-over on the comb of the stock. Through experimenting, I've noticed I can find two or three different positions that provide a sweet spot in terms of the whole scope view lighting up, but only one of these is really the 'one' to use. If you zero using one position, but then unconsciously use another in the field, you won't hit a barn door, due to parallax issues – which can be reduced although never eliminated completely. The different positions might impact on how you line up the crosshairs on the target, so it can become a crucial issue.

My rule of thumb is to shoulder the gun and practise with the position that comes most naturally, whilst being the one that has me looking as straight through the scope as possible, so that my eye is as square on to the eyepiece as I can get it. If you're new to shooting, it can be easy to ignore these subtle differences in technique. Do not force the position. Once you've decided on your ideal head position, make a point of remembering it and practise until it becomes so well trained that it becomes natural to return to the same position. This will add consistency to your zeroing, and your real-life shooting in the field. I've recently read somewhere that army snipers are trained always to ensure that they place their heads on the same spot on the stock, using the same orientation etc, to look down the scope. This ensures, as much as possible, that the crosshairs would always appear the same to the viewing eye. What I term a 'stock sweet spot' here, is apparently referred to by the army sniper as a 'spot weld'. Although a good scope, with parallax calibration should reduce these issues, it does not eliminate them, and inconsistencies in shouldering the gun will impact on downrange precision.

As a side point, the Tyrolean stock design – the prominent cheekpiece, covered earlier in relation to Venom Custom models – aids with consistent shouldering of the gun and head alignment. The idea is that the shooter's head always goes to the same place on the stock.

AIR SWEET SPOT

If shooting a PCP, it is important to know your air pressure sweet spot (discussed in another section). For my carbine S410K it is approximately 170–100 bar, and 180–90 bar on my Classic rifle. Only zero when in the sweet spot, otherwise you're just chasing rainbows and your gun will feel as if its consistency is all over the place.

Trigger Set-Up

I cannot stress how important a good trigger set-up is for precision shooting. Most modern air rifles are fitted with high-level, two-stage triggers, and there is no excuse not to have these calibrated for your own preferences. If in doubt, go to a reputable gun shop and ask for help and advice on how to set the trigger on your airgun. You do not want a trigger that needs so much pressure that your trigger finger pulls at the whole gun; nor do you want a dangerous 'hair trigger' which could go off too easily. You won't know how much better the trigger can be, if you do not explore it. If you're going to spend upwards of £500 on a top-end gun, get every penny-worth from it. It can transform your performance.

I like a light-to-medium pull weight with a little bit of travel on the first stage, before the second stage engages. This allows me to be precise in my pulling of the trigger. I also like a tad of second-stage movement before the trigger releases the pellet. Many target shooters will not like my trigger set-up, perhaps preferring more of a hair-trigger, but my preference allows me to back out of a shot if the optimal opportunity is quickly lost, and I was not fast enough to get the shot off. It allows me to be very considered when taking the shot, and I can often sit with a tad of pressure on the second stage whilst watching the quarry through the scope and waiting for the perfect shot to present itself, which will now just require the slightest bit of extra pull to execute. If the trigger is overly light, it feels too keen to fire and unpredictable, to me. If set too light, sometimes you might end up firing a shot long before you intended to and so completely

High-quality modern air rifles are fitted with adjustable two-stage triggers on which aspects of all stages (travel, 'bite point' and pull weight) can be altered. Explore how these can be optimised for your style of shooting. A well-adjusted trigger can vastly improve your performance and make your release of the pellet extremely intuitive.

GETTING STARTED   3

fluff the shot, or worse still, hit the animal before you were fully ready. It is all personal, but it's worth exploring your trigger set-up and have it so that it suits you and is consistent, safe, and predictable for you.

INITIAL STEPS

Using Chairgun, work out your optimal zero range and laser your target to this range. Set up a paper target, preferably one with crosshair markers on it. It is important to mount the target so that it is level, to ensure that the crosshair markers on it are truly aligned up/down and left/right. Load the gun and place firmly in the bench rest. If shooting a springer remember you will need to control the recoil with your forehand steadying the gun – do not just rest it unsupported because the airgun will kick before the pellet has the chance to leave the barrel. Ensure that the gun is level, and find your ideal position on the stock for looking down the scope. Align the crosshairs of the scope directly to those on the paper target, so that the centre of the crosshairs is placed in the bullseye of the target – this is why it is important that both the target and the scope are level. Ensure that the gun remains level and there is no canter during this process. Breathe slowly and squeeze a shot off. Note the position of the pellet hole – chances are you missed the bullseye, but alter nothing after one shot. Take another shot, possibly another two or three to establish a consistent landing point. Now adjust accordingly. If the pellets are landing low, then adjust the turret on the scope 'up' – or 'down' if landing high. If the pellet is landing to the left of the bullseye, then adjust the turret 'right' – or 'left' if the pellet is landing to the right. The number of clicks needed will depend on how far off the pellet is landing relative to the current position of the crosshairs and the zero distance.

Shoot and repeat. Again, do not alter the scope with every shot. Only alter the scope after two or three shots, assuming they land consistently off-target. You are zeroed when you are getting pellet on pellet, or touching groupings shot after shot into the bullseye region. Now put a host of shots through the gun to confirm the zero holds, and you have established your mechanical zero – where the scope crosshairs are as close as possible to the mechanical zero point of the gun/barrel itself. Once happy, take the gun off the bench rest. Now confirm the zero via a shooting stick, if you use them, or your shooting stances that give more freedom in the shouldering of the gun. I tend find little or no difference from the bench rest and so typically make no adjustments. However, you might, so it's important to make sure that if there are subtle differences between shooting from a bench rest and more natural free-shooting stances, you make the necessary adjustments, although these should be minor. You will not have the bench rest in the field! Once done, you will have a great deal of confidence in your zero and how it is set up. You are now zeroed and ready to go.

Taking Things A Step Further

Now that the gun is zeroed, you could explore your compensation points by setting targets at different ranges from your zero distance. To get a good feel for how the pellet is dropping with increased distance, set a target at 35 yards and 40 yards – they are easy to remember and represent typical hunting distances. Pick a magnification on the scope that would be the most typical one you would use in the field for most circumstances. Now, place the crosshairs on the bullseye at these different distances, and see how much the pellet drops to give you an indication of the curve in trajectory. If your scope is fitted with compensation points – mil-dots or equivalent – explore how they can be used as substitute zero points for the different distances.

You could use computer programs to help you establish the amount of hold over and the compensation points required for certain distances based on your individual combo, but it is always helpful to field test these concepts. Once done, you should end up with a really nice 'feel' for how your combo performs. Now that you've got this laid down in your mind, repeat in windy conditions and with targets at different elevations to take things to another level. However, if you know your gun is zeroed, don't alter this during these additional tests; remember, you're exploring degrees of compensation required for the current circumstances, so dial in the compensation required in your mind and use the reticle markings.

My Own Hunting Combinations

I've owned a number of airguns over the years, from a variety of manufacturers, and all for vermin/pest control. These have included various models from Webley & Scott – a Vulcan and a Sandwell-tuned Webley Longbow carbine, and Weihrauch – including a couple of legendary HW80s, but these days, I primarily shoot air

GETTING STARTED 3

rifles made by British airgun manufacturer, Air Arms (AA). My 'springer' of current choice is a rather nice MK III, TX200 Hunter Carbine (TX200 HC). These guns are also affectionately referred to as a 'T-Rex'. It is an awesome gun, a beacon of British engineering, and its merits are worthy of some discussion.

My T-Rex is a .22 carbine version of the TX200 series. The shorter barrel makes it lighter and to my mind, vastly improves the balance of the gun relative to its full-length brother. It utilises an under-lever design that allows for a fixed barrel. This means that assuming there is no fault with the gun, there will be no barrel drift or inconsistency in barrel alignment due to wear and tear, making it consistent and deadly – for life. Mine is fitted with a walnut stock. This is not just for aesthetic reasons. The walnut stock also reduces its weight by about a quarter of a pound, which again improves balance in the shoulder. It used to be said that a heavy spring gun was a quality spring gun. Maybe so, but remember you're going to be carrying it around all day and you have to be able to live with the weight. AA springers are known to be heavy, but by exploring tweaks like going for carbines and walnut stocks, this can make what might have been an unbalanced, nose-heavy gun, a real dream to use. My advice would also be to get your springer fitted with a sling and

My TX200 HC (T-Rex), in .22 calibre, fitted with a walnut stock. Without doubt, one of the finest spring guns and certainly the most consistent and precise springer I have ever owned. It's a bit of a looker as well.

swivels (gun strap) which makes life much easier in the field. Some airgun shooters really like heavy guns, some find them unbearable – which just goes to show, it is all subjective.

The T-Rex hardly recoils at all, making it probably as close to a PCP as any off-the-shelf springer can be. This also contributes to the achievable consistency of the T-Rex which is amazing. The trigger is a delightful two-stage unit, and tuned to perfection for my needs and style, straight from the factory. Spring guns have character; they put a smile on your face when you use them. You just pick them up, and go shooting. They are built like tanks and should give years of trouble-free enjoyment and shooting. I hope airgun manufacturers continue to invest in spring guns due to the very special experience they can give the shooter.

One thing I have always noticed with this gun is how hard it hits, which is very hard indeed. In fact, it hits so hard that when I first purchased it I was continually checking its muzzle energy because I didn't believe it was under 12 ft.lbs., although I'm pleased to say it was. You can be sure that if you invest in a gun like a T-Rex, you are getting a top-quality hunting rifle, capable of effectively culling vermin species at respectful distances, providing you do your part. The reputation of the T-Rex is legendary in the airgun community and is probably on a par, if not now superior to a similar legend, the HW77.

Another innovation from AA on their spring guns is the use of internal synthetic materials, reducing wear and making them smooth in operation. Both the T-Rex and its sister gun, the gorgeous AA Prosport, are regarded by airgun tuners as 'semi-tuned' out of the box and much closer to their ceiling level of performance than most, if not all other production units. Of course, improvements can always be made and the T-Rex is no exception; i.e., short-stroking is a particularly popular tuning for the Mk III, but these are far from absolutely necessary on new 'out of the box' units.

Target shooters often prefer the longer-barrel version of the T-Rex rather than the carbine, based on the claim that there is less muzzle flip than on the carbine, and this leads to better downrange precision. I would say the following: Firstly, I've never experienced any real muzzle flip on the carbine T-Rex – it is simply too heavy, and it shoots too sweetly. Of course, there is a small recoil kick, as there is on all springers, including the full-barrelled rifle version, but I'd never describe it as 'muzzle flip'. Secondly, I've never been aware of any noticeable advantages in the consistency of slot placement from the full-barrelled rifle relative to the carbine, over typical hunting distances. I'm not arguing that such differences do not exist, just that they

GETTING STARTED   3

are not present at typical hunting distances. Therefore, to the hunter, if differences are present they are just academic and will never come into play in the field. Thirdly, the superior handling of the carbine is not to be ignored by the hunter. The shorter barrel makes the gun ideal for hide-shooting, woodland shooting and shooting around farm buildings – these advantages are not unimportant. Of course, these are subjective factors, but I report them here as honestly as I can. Shoot what works for you, but be aware of these issues when considering a purchase.

As well as my T-Rex I own two PCPs, both from Air Arms. These are, an AA S410K and an AA S410 Classic. The S410K is fitted with a stunning tiger-stripe walnut sporter stock, and is a dream to shoot – very fast into the shoulder and deadly. Although I am a competent shot, I am certainly nowhere near as good as those competing in target shooting, but with this gun I can achieve groupings under, or no bigger than the diameter of a five-pence piece out to 35 yards from a supported position, and touching groups out to 40 yards. It is extremely consistent, giving tight groups at very respectable distances. I like the bolt-action – smooth as butter – the

My tuned AA S410K (the 'Tiger') in .22 calibre, fitted with a stunning, tiger-stripe walnut stock. This gun is compact, deadly, silent, and super-fast into the shoulder. Ideal for all shooting scenarios, but comes into its own league when stalking in dense woodland and around farm buildings. I've shot many PCPs over the years, but for me, the S410 is arguably one of the finest all-round PCP hunting airguns one can own. This gun is over 15 years old, is used regularly, and has never let me down in the field. It's my 'go to' unit and we've shared countless forays together.

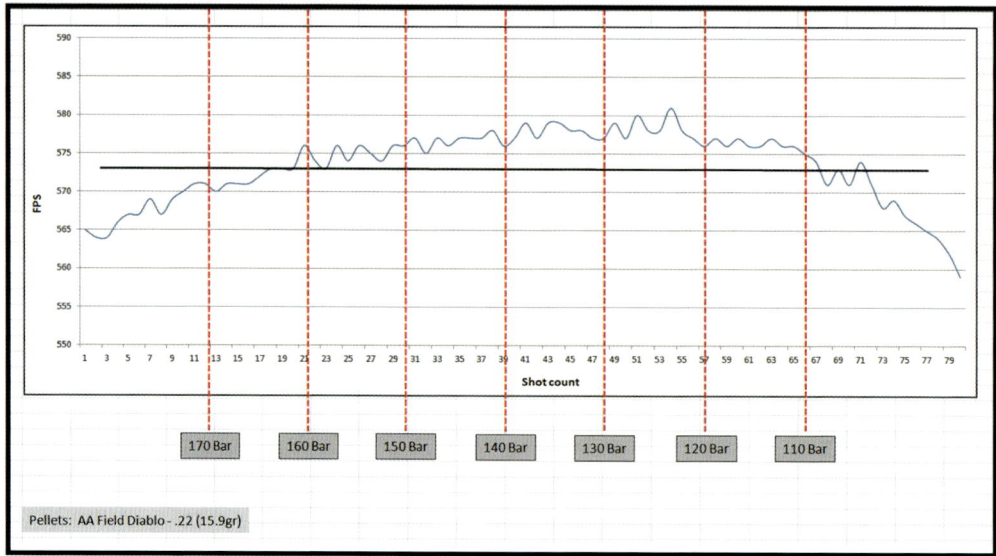

The power curve and efficiency (blue waveform) of my tuned S410K from a fill of 180 bar with drops in pressure in approximate 10 bar steps. In terms of the chronograph results, it suggests that there are around 60 shots within 1.5% of the peak velocity (the sweet spot – black horizontal line). This sweet spot begins around 165 bar (574 fps), and ends a few shots after 110 bar. In terms of testing with targets, at 28 yards to 40 yards, there is no significant difference in the zero of the gun from 170–100 bar, thus giving more like 65 highly consistent shots. At no point in the sweet spot does the gun drop below 11.60 ft.lbs., and at no point across the entire 80-shot test string does it drop below 11.04 ft.lbs.

10-shot magazine and the whole operation of the S410 series is very transparent, extremely intuitive, and easy to learn. This gun is currently fitted with a Hawke Airmax 30, 4-16 x 50mm scope which has crisp glassware, a nice thin reticle design (AMX-IR: not too cluttered) with clear compensation points for hold over, which is important for a .22 calibre airgun. The scope has an accurate side parallax adjustment and a brightness-adjustable illuminated reticle for shooting in woodland in low light, and the 50mm objective lens allows for lots of light to help with shooting at dusk. It's a nice scope, although to be honest, a tad on the heavy side.

I have had this air rifle tuned and 'fettled' by Mike Rudge, of the AirgunForum (AGF), who is an expert on Air Arms products. All the perishable seals in the gun were replaced; striker rails, hammer polished to a mirror finish and lubricated, springs

GETTING STARTED | 3

checked for tension and strength, ports checked and cleaned and the power curve set, shimmed and calibrated. The maximum power it generated, with AA Field Diabolo pellets, peaked at 11.7 ft.lbs., and it gave around 60 shots within 1.5% of this peak – the sweet spot. After tuning, Mike put a full shot-string through the gun, which revealed an average of 3fps shot-by-shot variation between 165 bar to 110 bar– the new sweet spot – with a maximum variation of 8fps over the entire sweet spot. I am delighted with how this gun continues to perform, over a decade after I purchased it. More recently, I have had this airgun fitted with a true two-stage trigger (3-sear), which has improved how this gun feels and shoots. I've also updated the moderator to an AA Q-Tec and there were noticeable improvements to be had relative to the standard moderator I've had on the gun.

My other PCP is also a S410, but a more recent Classic, full rifle 'F' version, fitted with a walnut thumbhole stock. In the shoulder the stock feels absolutely exquisite and it is hard not to do a good job – the ergonomics seem to help with head alignment, at least for me. I have calibrated the butt plate to give a nice alignment in the shoulder, and once in position, the gun feels absolutely delightful. It is effortless to shoot. This rifle came fitted with a true, two-stage trigger as standard, and once set up, was a joy to shoot. This air rifle has also been fully tuned by Mike Rudge, as detailed for the carbine, providing very comparable and impressive results, but over a longer shot count (75 shots).

AA S410 Classic, fitted with a walnut thumbhole stock. The thumbhole stock is incredibly comfortable. This gun is extremely sweet to shoot, easily capable of pellet-on-pellet groups out to 35 yards, and beyond in the right hands. It is the perfect ambush rifle.

3 THE AIRGUNNER'S COMPANION

My Air Arms S410 Classic fitted with a custom high-grade American Black walnut Tyrolean stock (Courtesy of Gary Cane Gun Stocks). Although absolutely stunning to look at, customisations like this are not just for aesthetic reasons. This airgun is extremely well balanced and the distinctive Tyrolean cheek-piece ensures consistent head positioning for looking down the telescopic sight. As this has been custom made for my personal measurements, it is extremely comfortable and natural in the shoulder. The hand-cut chequering on the fore end and pistol grip also provide a very positive connection to the gun in the demanding conditions out in the field. The combination of a highly tuned Air Arms rifle and stunning craftsmanship from Gary Cane provides an exceptional shooting experience.

GETTING STARTED

In recent times, I've tended to take the full rifle out for hide and fixed ambush shooting, and the carbine for more mobile stalking, woodland or farm shooting, but again, there is no need for any hard and fast rules here.

I have carried out extensive testing on all my airguns to establish what I consider to be the best hunting pellet. I have also explored the different head sizes, as well as different brands. For example, AA Field Diabolos work well and are the pellet of

ABOVE: *This represents what I consider to be an excellent level of dispersion for a .22 calibre PCP at typical hunting distances. The target was shot 10 times (a full magazine) at 35 yards, and many shots went into the same hole. This represents what shooters mean by 'touching groups' (cloverleaf patterns). For me, this is about as good as I can shoot. The shots were taken from a seated position. The centre-mass spread is much less than the diameter of a five-pence piece.*

Once you have identified your preferred pellet, zeroed your gun and put the practice in, a modern air rifle should be able to give excellent results at respectable distances.

RIGHT: *In this photo there is one flier, but the centre mass of the other 19 shots are tight and located around the bullseye.*

BELOW RIGHT: *The target involved an adjustment in the zero, where the first three or four shots fell low and to the left until corrected. Targets were placed at 38 yards and shot from a seated and supported position. The centre mass spread of the accurate shots is below that of the diameter of a five-pence piece.*

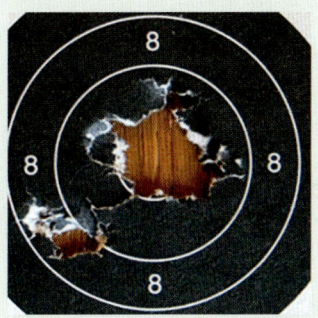

3 THE AIRGUNNER'S COMPANION

Six shots from the S410K at a target placed 33 yards away. The radial lines on these targets are approximately 8mm apart. As can be seen, five of the six shots fall within the '4' ring. For reference, note a five-pence piece has a diameter of around 18mm, a 10-pence piece around 24mm, and a two-pence piece around 26mm. All shots are well below the diameter of the five-pence piece, thus the level of dispersion in the grouping is excellent for hunting.

choice for both my PCPs (tightest groups), followed closely by JSB Exact Jumbo. These pellets like my barrels. All these pellets allow for the clinical placement of the pellet to a high level. I also explore my compensation points – for holding over – at increased distances and for different magnifications in the scope.

These are the hunting combinations that I take with me out on my shooting forays, and they are extremely effective at the job they have to do. The take-home message is; buy from quality manufacturers, keep your guns well-serviced and do not over-fiddle with them. If they are shooting fine, leave them alone and concentrate on other aspects of your skills. Do your bit to learn how your gun, scope and pellet combinations perform. Job done – you are now ready for the field.

POINT OF IMPACT (POI) ON LIVE QUARRY

If you are considering shooting at live vermin species, then it is important to know where to place your pellet on them. If you have put your practice in and have a good set-up, you should enjoy good precision shooting, but where do we aim for? The site where you intend the pellet to hit is referred to as the Point of Impact or POI. There is an important facet to thinking about POIs on wild animals that is

RIGHT: *A schematic illustration of a 3-dimensional POI. Try to think of the pellet's path as passing 'through' the organism and not just as a surface entry point. Placing a pellet so that it causes maximal atrophy 'inside' the organism as it passes into the tissue will optimise the efficacy of the damage done by the shot. Here, the path illustrated inside the schematic brain (dotted arrow) illustrates the route. If this were a brain shot, the dotted arrow should be thought of as passing through the bulk of the brain or brain stem, after and beyond the surface POI.*

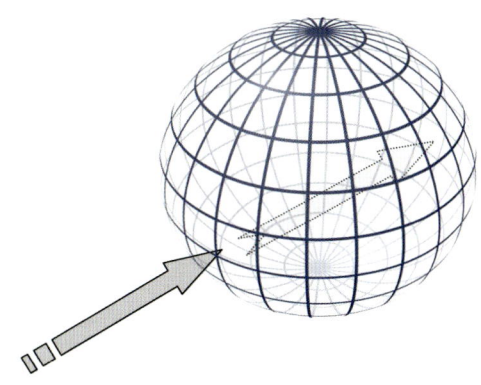

RIGHT: *Here is the same principle illustrated again, but now showing that at steep angles, even though the surface contact point may seem to be reasonably placed, the internal path through the brain actually misses the bulk of it. Here, the dotted arrow needs to be much lower to be passing through the bulk of the critical tissue in order to cause maximum internal atrophy. The only way to achieve this is to compensate with a lower entry point (POI) into the brain.*

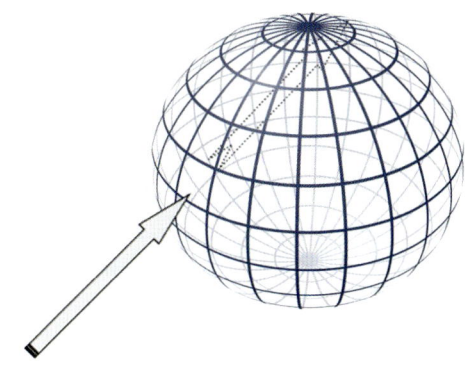

not always discussed in hunting circles. To me, it is best to think of POIs as a three-dimensional thing. Many people only think about POIs in terms of the contact point on the surface of the animal, but this suggests that there is no consideration for the path the pellet takes inside the animal. For live quarry, it is more useful to visualise an imaginary path for the pellet going through the animal in a straight line. This is even more the case when shooting at extreme angles – high into trees, or from a high point down onto the ground, for example, or if the animal presents a sub-optimal angle. If necessary, adjust the surface POI accordingly to ensure that the full path of the pellet induces maximum internal atrophy. So, by thinking about the path and angle of the pellet, travelling through tissue, you will be less likely to miss completely the critical area you are targeting deep inside the animal, and this is why thinking in three dimensions is so important.

As with many things in the airgun community, POI on animals is a hotly debated and somewhat confused topic, with some hunters arguing for brain shots all of the time, and others for heart shots. Of course, the reality is somewhat more complicated than that; the role of context and shooting situation, as well as the animal in question, needs to be considered here because although a brain shot could well be optimal, sometimes the heart shot might be effective – and that's not to mention throat shots, which can also be highly effective and humane.

I have a view on this that requires some discussion to put things into their proper context. For me, hunting with sub-12 ft.lbs. air rifles, means brain shots are the preferred and optimal shot. They are the gold standard and made a whole lot easier by the technology available to the modern hunter, i.e. precision rifles, pellets, scopes, rangefinders, and so on. To stretch things further, the gold standard of brain shots, if at all possible, is a brain-stem shot, perhaps only really possible on some larger quarry like rabbits or squirrels. If you can place your pellet cleanly into the brain or brain stem, with a full-powered air rifle, over typical hunting distances, then the animal will be humanely and instantly dispatched – no question about it – end of story. This is the advice I give to all newcomers and it is what I practise myself in the field. We could end the discussion here and the information above would be entirely accurate and useful. Where confusion emerges is that on occasion alternative POIs might need to be considered.

There are a number of reasons why brain shots should be considered the optimal POI. The brain itself is vital for life – it drives heartbeat etc – and so impacting on its ability to sustain life should ensure humane culling. Another really good reason for recommending brain shots is that they are easier to visualise on the animal. In most cases there will be visual 'landmarks' and their spatial layout can be used to mark the POI easily – the alignment between the back of the eyes and the base of the ears, and so on. Although a brain shot is a small target, these landmarks can actually make brain shots easier because they are more clearly delineated on the animal. Modern air rifles are capable of groupings below the diameter of a five-pence piece out to 35–40 yards, which when combined with an appropriate POI is sufficient for clinical brain shots on all pest species.

However, brain shots themselves can be demanding for other reasons. The weather conditions – wind or rain – might impact on your aim, causing you to

GETTING STARTED

miss the small intended target area that can be even more demanding at increasing distance. In addition, the head of a woodpigeon, for example, is small and rarely still when feeding, which make such shots extremely challenging. I have heard this argument many times from people advocating a POI directed at the larger heart cavity area, and I'm unconvinced by these arguments. If distance is an issue, then stalk or decoy the animal into a more reasonable range. If the wind is excessive, then don't shoot beyond short distances in those circumstances. Sometimes things work against you and make the potential shot sub-optimal and in such cases, when little can be done to swing things in your favour, then the quarry should live to fight another day. Finally, you do not have to shoot feeding pigeons. Wait for them to return to their sitty trees and I can assure you, their heads don't move for hours. I'm only slightly joking here!

The reality is that whilst brain shots are indeed the gold standard and should always be chosen whenever possible as the optimum POI, there are some exceptions that can occur in the field to suggest other alternatives might be superior for that species, and under the particular circumstances presented to you. For example, for the woodpigeon, a throat POI can also be ideal and luckily there is a white-collar marking in the neck area that signals the aiming spot. It is important to avoid the 'crop', the little fatty sack where they house feed. This is located in the upper chest area. When full you can see it as a slightly swollen section in the feathers. Do not shoot into the crop, thinking you are targeting the chest or neck, it is like tough leather, airgun pellets will not penetrate through it and the bird will just fly off, injured.

Studying the basic anatomy of animals will help to inform on the optimal POI and how to visualise its position on a living animal.

Grey squirrels are renowned to be tough, and their heads are a small target at 30 yards. They are also harder to kill than any rabbit, despite being a third of the size. For me, squirrels should always be brain shots and a well-considered POI into the brain is required to drop them cleanly. For side-on shots, in your mind draw a line between the back of the eye, and base of the ear. Bisect this line and slightly bias your POI a bit more toward the base of the ear, but not directly under it. This is the point to aim for – it's not only a brain shot, but is also highly likely to take out the brain stem. I find squirrels drop particularly well when shot in the top of the head as they scurry up or down tree trunks, presenting the hunter with an aerial view of their heads. In these cases, in your mind draw a line between the ears, bisect the line, and shoot just a smidge in front of it, which will be just behind the eyes and just in front of the base of the ears. Again, you will take the brain clean out. When done properly, Mr Squirrel will drop like a stone, with no drama.

For rabbits, brain shots are again optimal, and I personally prefer brain shots on rabbits whenever possible. I've also changed my preferred 'exact' spot in recent years. My original POI was to simply draw an imaginary line between the back of the eye and the base of the ear, from a side on view of the head, then bisect this line and shoot at that spot, halfway between eye and base of the ear, with a light bias toward the eye. It is a good POI, humane and effective. However, I now shoot slightly lower than the imaginary line and slightly more toward the base of the ear. This appears to drop them more soundly, and I believe this is due to taking out more of the brain stem than the central brain itself. The brain-stem contains more vital parts for life including those responsible for heartbeat and breathing. The downside is that this more optimal shot is closer to the back of the head and the chance of a complete miss is increased. Nonetheless, I'd always prefer that outcome over one in which the animal is not humanely dispatched.

Although not my preferred shot, in some cases heart shots are certainly tenable for rabbits and they can drop very cleanly from such a POI. However, with rabbits, heart shots can ruin the meat in the upper body, in case you wanted to cook with it. There isn't much meat on the upper body region of the rabbit, but all those rib bones and joints contain a lot of flavour so even if you cannot retrieve that much meat from this area, I still like to cook with it for flavour in stews and pies. Furthermore,

A woodpigeon sitting square on. Which would be the most optimal POI in this case? One option might be to go for the eye in the hope that the pellet will also take out the brain on its way through the skull – the bulk of the brain is behind the eye. It's possible, but the upward angle might mean that the pellet will skim over the top of the bulk of the brain (visualise it in 3D – see text). In this case, an alternative throat shot marked by the white-feather collar would also be a good choice. Remember to avoid the 'crop' on woodpigeons.

A more side-on view of a woodpigeon. A clean brain shot is much more viable here, right behind the eye, but again, some compensation might be needed to ensure that the pellet takes out most of the brain and does not skim past the bulk of it due to the elevated angle. A throat shot is also certainly viable as well, and arguably, in this case the optimal POI. A chest shot is tricky because the branch in front of the crest of the wing might obscure the optimal route into the heart cavity, and remember – the trajectory of the pellet is curved and might hit the branch first. If in doubt, do not take that particular shot.

the skill required to locate the heart accurately is much harder, and this is one reason that I do not recommend these shots to beginners. There are no easily recognisable landmarks on rabbits indicating the ideal route to the heart.

Beginners must resist the temptation to shoot to the centre body mass to improve chances of a hit. This will not kill and can be quite cruel, and is one reason that I don't recommend heart shots for beginners because they often just take body shots instead. Never shoot any living animal in the gut with an air rifle. It will not kill the animal humanely. In some cases the pellet will just remain in the animal with no adverse effects; in worse cases it will leave them to die a slow and painful death many hours later. Conscientious hunters owe it to themselves and their quarry to avoid unnecessary pain and injury. If in doubt – brain shots only. If you miss, you miss, and the animal lives to fight another day. Do not experiment with POIs on live animals. Do your homework on the anatomy of the quarry of interest and put your practice in on the target range at inanimate paper targets to hone your technique.

To summarise, brain shots are the gold standard and should be the preferred POI if at all possible. Throat shots can also be extremely effective with the desired result instantaneous. Heart shots can work but only if you know exactly where to aim in order to target the chest cavity. Never shoot any animal in the stomach. It is unlikely that such a POI would be effective even with a high-energy FAC-rated air rifle. Taking on shots, without any knowledge of anatomy or optimal POIs is inhumane and has no place in true hunting. It is also worth remembering that sometime the perfect shot never presents itself and alas we are outwitted by our quarry.

THE AIRGUNNER'S COMPANION

THE IMPORTANCE OF CONTINUED TARGET PRACTICE

Getting good at shooting an air rifle is only half the battle. Staying good is the other half and it does not happen by chance – it requires constant attention. As well as getting to know your combo, hunters need to maintain a motor/muscle memory in order to get the best out of hunting. Knowledge of how your set-up performs is the first step. Then learn how your trigger 'feels' and how to shoulder your gun correctly so that your face meets the cheekpiece in the same place every time, and that eye to scope alignment is consistent. These processes need to be practised so that they become as intuitive as possible and you no longer need to think about it. Shooting from different stances and positions, at different distances and angles should be practised so that nothing surprises you in the field. As a consequence of all this, most hunters will either have a practice range in their garden, on the farmland, or be a member of an airgun club. Hunters might also be interested in target shooting competitions, but even if they're not, hunters still need target practice to gain proficiency and maintain a sufficient level of shooting skill.

If I haven't been shooting for a few weeks, I notice it immediately when I pick the gun up and have a few practice shots at a target. It matters not that I have been shooting for over 35 years, the consistency in my shooting will have deteriorated – albeit marginally – and so a few test shots and thoughts about technique serve as a timely reminder until it all starts coming back to me and my performance returns. It is often the case that the last time you were down the range you were drilling single holes at 35 yards, but don't expect that proficiency to hang around without practice. Staying sharp requires dedicated practice. Hunting, on its own, is not always sufficient because you might go days before a reasonable series of opportunities present themselves, and hunting in the field is not the place to experiment with your technique.

SHOOTING TECHNIQUE: SOME BASIC TIPS

I am certainly no target shooter. However, I am aware of the small idiosyncrasies that creep into all our styles of shooting, and I've thought long and hard over the years about what suits my style more. Do not feel you need to shoot a certain way if it feels uncomfortable or unnatural to you. What comes naturally is most important, unless it truly leads to bad habits. The issue of canter is a good example of a clear bad habit.

Canter is when the airgun is not being held level – either the left- or right-hand side of the gun being higher than the other side. It can occur very easily when looking through the scope at a landscape that is not level. We tend to be influenced by the horizontal plane of the environment and subconsciously adjust the orientation of the airgun in the shoulder to match what we see, but the truth is, what we see in the environment is itself rarely level. The magnitude of this can be slight, but will have a big impact on your shot placement and more so with increasing distance.

One useful tip when practising is to get a friend to stand behind you and correct your alignment when shouldering the airgun, if it's not obvious to you that you are cantering the gun. Always make sure the airgun is seated correctly in your shoulder. There are lots of little steps in shouldering the airgun, so make the whole process of standing and shouldering is almost automatic by practising all these elements.

RIGHT: *Different configurations of how to hold and steady the front of the airgun. In the picture on the right, the forehand is at the end of the stock. By being closer to the muzzle one might argue that it helps to control the front end of the gun – however, the leading arm lacks support from the rest of the body*

RIGHT: *In the picture on the right, the forehand/elbow is tucked in closer to the body and gains additional support from the body. I find both comfortable. Explore and see what works for you and then practise that hold. Make sure you remain consistent once in the field.*

3 THE AIRGUNNER'S COMPANION

Elbow up, or elbow down when the airgun is in the shoulder? Again, explore your technique and make sure that you practise the one with which you are most comfortable. For me, lifting my elbow creates a nice pocket for the butt of the stock to sit into, and dropping my elbow creates my chest muscle to pop the gun forward an inch or two – though it is still very comfortable. It is important to be aware of how such factors could be impacting on your technique – and it can be hard to monitor all these different facets once the gun is in the shoulder. Use what works for you, but be consistent in practice and in the field. Note: The rake on the pistol grip of the stock can also impact on what 'feels' natural, which means you might shoulder different airguns in very different ways. I find both comfortable.

Another issue refers to shooting 'thumb up' or 'thumb down'. I know a few target shooters who use a standard sporter stock, but like to shoot 'thumb up'. What this refers to is the position of your thumb, on your trigger hand, on the grip of the stock. Shooting 'thumb up' means the thumb on this hand does not go all the way around the grip, but rides up the back of the grip – as if to give someone a thumb up. Some find this more comfortable and argue that it allows for a better trigger pull technique, by imagining squeezing between the trigger fingers and the thumb. Again, it is all subjective and likely influenced by the physical characteristics of the shooter's hand, the rake angle on the grip of the stock and the position of the trigger. Nonetheless, explore what works for you and try to settle on a consistent shooting style.

4 Hunting: Permissions

GAINING PERMISSIONS

When starting out it can be tricky getting that first shooting permission. You are often asking a complete stranger not only to trust you, but also to do so with a firearm on their land. One method is to write to farmers and landowners to introduce yourself. Explain your request, be very cordial, provide your contact details and wait. You might also mention you are a member of an association like BASC, and that you are fully insured. If I were a landowner I wouldn't let anyone on my land unless they were insured. You want to mention the vermin species you are interested in culling – do not expect landowners to have detailed knowledge on these matters – and invite an initial informal interview, to have a chat and possibly set things up. A self-addressed envelope should be provided and would show you are being considerate. You might not get a reply for a while, and do not be disheartened if you get a few rejections first. Be patient.

If the chance of an initial meeting is offered, don't show up in full camouflage gear with your guns on your back. This sends the wrong message. It is also not a wedding, so there's no need to overdo things either. Just dress normally and be respectful. First impressions count. If things go well, ask about the land boundary and if the landowner can show you the limits of the land, or mark them on a map for you. If you get permission on the day, it is not a good idea just to run to the car and get the guns out. Show you're more considerate than that and go for a walk around the land in order to get to know it. Get a feel for the land and the challenges it poses. Take binoculars and scan the area.

If the permission involves a farmhouse and buildings, ask whether the farmer has a family, and any children running and playing around the farm buildings. What about pets – dogs, cats? What about feral cats, which some farmers have to help control the rats? Are these present on the farm? You simply need to know what might be around, and you need a constant awareness of it. What type of livestock does the farmer have – a herd of cattle that will be brought in for milking at certain times of the day, or sheep, lamb pens, etc? Are there any problems with aggressive bulls or boisterous bullocks that you need to know about? The last thing you want to do is enter a field and become the object of an aggressive bull's attention. Are there any horses on the land? They can be quite skittish at times. Pigs will often mean rats, but ask about shooting near the pigpens. Are there any times of the day or year the farmer really needs you there, or definitely does not want you around?

How does the farmer want you to dispose of any culled quarry? Many have incinerators on site these days, and it might be appropriate to throw things in there, but ask about the procedure they'd like you to follow. Even for things like rabbits, it might not be a good idea to come from the fields and walk right past the farmhouse swinging dead rabbits in front of the farmer's children or grandchildren. It's important the farmer knows of your successes, but there are more elegant ways to do this than displaying dead carcases. Although it's your hobby, it is the farmer's livelihood, so engage in regular consultations and be respectful of his/her wishes.

SHARED PERMISSIONS

On some of my shooting land, there are others who also have permission to shoot, but some are there to take foxes, some to cull the deer. I'm often the only airgunner, or one of only two airgunners, and we communicate closely when we know we are around at the same time. This is a very harmonious situation, or at least it can be if sensible people are involved. Many hunters are very protective of the land they shoot, and this is understandable. Things can also get very political. However, if the land is extensive, containing many vermin and game species, then there is often enough shooting for everyone and no one needs to step on each other's toes.

Airguns are ideal for small pest quarry and vermin and not suitable for things like foxes and deer. Similarly, cartridge-based rifles and shotguns are a little too excessive for some of the smaller vermin quarry and obviously ideally suited for the larger species. Many landowners and farmers are not overly aware that they could let airgunners on their land without undermining what the shotgun syndicate or deer shooters are paying for, so it often helps to put everyone's mind at rest if the incoming airgunner states explicitly that they only want to shoot small vermin or pests, and will not encroach on other species at all. In fact, this can be made explicit in any shooting permission agreement, and shows that you are committed to

HUNTING: PERMISSIONS 4

forming a clear understanding between everyone involved. You take the rats, rabbits, woodpigeon, mink, and grey squirrels, and let the others stick to the pheasants. On a shared permission, do not violate this agreement.

LISTEN TO THE LANDOWNER

It is important to listen to the landowner once you get your permission to shoot on his/her land. It might be a very relaxed gig where you can take a walk over the land whenever you feel like it – nothing overly serious – just enjoy yourself, respect the livestock and boundaries, and get cracking. However, although for most of us airgunning is a hobby, it is often the case that there is a job to be done and the landowner wants it doing. You might well be a volunteer, and doing things in your spare time, but the idea is that pests are going to be controlled so it is important to take it seriously.

We might fancy hitting the rabbits, but if chats with the landowner reveal that the rats appear to be more of a concern, then priorities need to be modified. Different issues can emerge at different times in the year, and the landowner will let you know, but it's important to be his/her eyes and ears on the land, and sometimes make pre-emptive strikes on a particular quarry, in certain locations. The farmer will thank you for it. After a while, the landowner will feel great when they know you're on-site keeping an eye on things, and you will become a welcome addition to the working farm. This is also how word of mouth spreads and other permissions or projects can occur in the future.

DOING YOUR RESEARCH: ASSESS THE CHALLENGES POSED BY THE LAND

Establishing the landowner's boundaries that demark the land you have permission to shoot, is the first thing to do once you have secured the shooting permission. You must never cross these boundaries and your shots toward any quarry species must never cross them – unless you have permission for the land on the other side.

Different land permissions pose different problems. Dense woodland, perched on the side of a steep fellside is a very different proposal to large, flat open fields. The presence of streams, becks and rivers, public footpaths, bridleways, and buildings need to be identified and considered. During this process, it is also important to gain an understanding of the various routes around farm buildings, the noise of gates and how they lock, etc. Establish entry points to fields, the presence of stiles … are there any weak points in fences and gates that should not be touched? Examine the coverage given by hedgerows, trees, buildings, machinery and so on. It might be quiet obvious where the rabbits are, but how do you get close to them? It is also helpful to have an understanding of where the sun rises and sets and the implications from that; a setting sun on a summer evening will provide lots of shadows cast by hedgerows into a field, and these shadows could be used to get very close to rabbits. Get a feel for these sorts of issues.

DEVELOP A STRATEGY

Some jobs are simple and basic, and a relaxed walk-over is often all that is needed That's great because you can decide on a whim what you might target, or just walk over the land and see what pops up, but some shoots are more serious and the problems more severe. They need careful considered attention and the development of a strategy. The first decision might be to think about which quarry to hit, and whereabouts on the land – unless the landowner has given explicit instructions on this matter. This decision might also be mediated by what time of year it is and what this means for the different quarry; i.e., mating season, pregnancy, etc. Should I hit the rabbits in the farm buildings or the rabbits in the top field? … the rats in the feed shed? … the pigeons in the big barn? … the rooks in the field?

The next decision might be, how? What method am I going to use? I can simply hide and ambush, use decoys, or for rats you could put some bait or feed down for a few days to establish a feeding place, and then, on the third or fourth day, be ready in a hidden, but ideally pre-chosen ambusher's hideout. In contrast, you could try lamping. What about night vision? Should you start by preparing some hides? What time should you arrive in order to get into position? What is the weather forecast? What time does it get light or dark? There is a lot to think about when developing an effective strategy, but it is great fun and all part of the skill of effective vermin control. Observe the animal behaviour on the land. What does it tell you? Are the rabbits out in more numbers in the early morning, or late evening, or both? What to do – early

HUNTING: PERMISSIONS — 4

morning, through the day, at dusk, and at night? The take-home message here is that it is not always the case to simply show up with your air rifle and just randomly meander around the land. Have a game plan. Chance favours the prepared mind!

SHOOTING ALONE OR WITH PARTNERS

Shooting with partners can be effective if the land is vast, or the problem a large one. An extra pair of hands can be useful. There are two basic scenarios when shooting in pairs; people can team up and shoot together in physical proximity to each other, or split up to different regions on the land. With the latter scenario, there needs to be a constant awareness of where each shooter is, and an agreement never to shoot anything that means pointing the gun in the other person's direction. Communication is key here. Pre-arranged rules of the areas to be covered before meeting up in a few hours' time is a good idea if partners are going to split up. It is also important only to go shooting with sensible people who know how to handle an airgun and are safe. Never put yourself in an ambiguous situation in regard to other people, and never take friends on to land without permission from the landowner. Make sure you can vouch for your friend. He or she might well get your permission revoked if they are not sensible.

5 Hunting: Equipment

GETTING SERIOUS

The airgun, scope and pellets are all one needs to start hunting, but there is a wider set of equipment that should be thought of as ranging from essential to generally useful. The list below is by no means extensive, but covers some of the main contenders that should be in your rucksack once you have decided to be serious about hunting with airguns. If your interest grows over the years, your kit will grow as well.

KNIVES AND KNIFE-SHARPENING KITS

A hunting knife is an essential piece of kit. Some hunters have different knives for different jobs. For example, they might have a specific knife for animal work, and another knife for more general field work. The former can have a small, thin and sharp blade, which is ideal for the simple job it has to do; i.e. making basic incisions, paunching, hocking rabbit legs, and so on, but little else. The latter can also have a small, sharp blade, although it might need a thicker blade to improve its general robustness for a broader range of tasks. Personally, I prefer a general all-purpose knife, one that is suited to all these tasks and so, not for the first time, it becomes a trade-off in an attempt to balance these opposing forces. You certainly do not need anything with a massive blade that looks like it should be in the movies!

I prefer fixed-blade knives for all my hunting and fieldwork. Over the years, I have accrued a number of knives and currently use around four rather nice ones with good quality blades; an EKA JoF7; a Helle 'Fire' model; a Helle 'Aldren' model, and a TBS 'Boar' knife fitted with a high-grade Bohler K720 carbon tool steel blade. The EKA has a hollow-grind blade, and both Helle models and the TBS have what is known as a 'Scandinavian' blade grind – or a 'Scandi', and curly birch handles.

The TBS knife comes with a 25 micron, fine-diamond sharpening stone and a fire-steel if you require it for starting fires in the outdoors, or on camping trips.

HUNTING: EQUIPMENT   5

Top Right: *Helle 'Aldren'.*
Middle: *Helle 'Fire'.*
Right: *EKA JoF7. All are excellent knives with high-quality blades.*

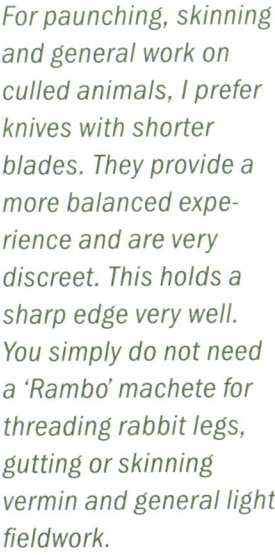

For paunching, skinning and general work on culled animals, I prefer knives with shorter blades. They provide a more balanced experience and are very discreet. This holds a sharp edge very well. You simply do not need a 'Rambo' machete for threading rabbit legs, gutting or skinning vermin and general light fieldwork.

This knife is built like a tank and should outlive me! The handle helps with grip, even when your hands are covered in gunk from paunching rabbits. All of these blades are more than capable of holding a very sharp edge for a long period of time, although this can depend on what you use them for. If looked after correctly, a quality knife should last you a lifetime. With fixed blade knives there is no locking mechanism to have to lubricate, or which can fail over time – it has happened to me.

A quality hunting knife should not cost the earth, but at the same time 'cheap as chips' is not the way to go either. It's going to have a hard life – let's hope – and needs to be up to the challenges you will throw at it year after year. All of these knives have features that make them attractive to hunters. Other brands such as Mora and Opinel are favoured by hunters and represent excellent value for money, although mine never seemed to last more than a few years, at best, hence the investment in more serious knives. Don't get me wrong, a five-quid knife from the hardware store is more than up to the job, but not for decades.

No matter how good a knife is, it will need sharpening from time to time, or some form of blade-edge maintenance will be required. For when out in the field, or if just a light maintenance of the blade edge is required, a combination of a pocket 'pull-through' sharpener fitted with ceramic rods can be very useful, coupled to finishing off with a leather strop. Sometimes, this is all that is required. I really like the 'FireSharp', a hand-held sharpener by EKA. The angle of the rods is 22-degrees, making it ideally suitable for my EKA knife which, with its hollow-grind blade, can be tricky to sharpen on a stone.

If necessary, I treat my blades to a more involved sharpening routine. For the non-carbon steel blades, I use a dual grain Japanese water stone. The lower grain numbers refer to a coarser stone and conversely, the higher number refers to a finer grain. For basic sharpening and shining an edge I use a 1000/5000 stone. If blades are in poor condition, a 500/800 grain is more suitable for initial sharpening. If nervous about learning how to use a sharpening stone on your hunting knife, buy some cheap knives to practise on – or even some kitchen cutlery! I finish my blades off by stropping them on leather or a newspaper, which contains fine grains of carbon in the dark print, and this works well for adding the very final touches to the blade. In fact, simply stropping a blade after use is often all that is needed to maintain a really sharp edge on a quality blade. An edge of around 22 degrees is ideal for hunting knives – the smaller the angle the sharper the edge, the higher the angle the more sturdy the edge will be – so, as with so many things, it's a balancing act between these factors.

HUNTING: EQUIPMENT 5

Always observe the law regarding the carrying of knives. It is not illegal to have a fixed-blade knife on your person, providing there is a genuine reason for you carrying it. Shooting and fishing would count, while you are doing these acts. Walking down the high street would not count as a viable reason. If you carry a knife in the car, to and from shooting, place it in a secure spot in the boot, in the rucky, and out of sight and easy reach. Remember to remove it from the car when not shooting.

SHOOTING STICKS AND BIPODS

The steadier one can hold the gun, the less variability in barrel position when shooting. This has the knock-on consequence of leading to improved precision in shot placement at increased distances. Bipods, which are attached to the gun toward the front of the stock, can provide a lot of stability and are a favoured choice for many hunters. In more recent times, shooting sticks have also become very popular, and both do similar jobs in different ways. The downsides of a bipod are that it is attached to the gun, will add to its weight and distort its balance if other unsupported shots are attempted. In addition, to benefit from many bipods it can mean that shots need to be taken from the prone position – unless the bipod is adjustable for other shots. Although a very accurate shooting posture, prone shooting might not always be suitable or desirable – the ground could be soaking and muddy and completely uninviting for the shooter.

On the other hand, shooting sticks provide the shooter with more flexibility in shooting stances. They can provide support over a wider range of angles, allowing you to shoot down at rats, or up at pigeons, with ease. They are light and well made – in fact, you can make your own if you'd prefer. The main downside of a shooting stick is that it is something extra to carry and so slightly more cumbersome to walk

A Primos tripod trigger-stick is a handy tool when hide shooting for a few hours.

around with. My current stick of choice is the Primos Tripod Trigger Stick. It's a well-built piece of kit; light, yet strong, and the trigger system means that the legs just drop silently when you pull the trigger ,giving quick support. I have the tripod version, which can also be used as a monopod if you keep the legs tied together, so there are plenty of options for how it can be used to best effect.

Trigger sticks work particularly well with a 'sit and ambush' strategy. One tip, when I pull the trigger on the stick, three legs descend to the ground, so when setting up the stick, I try to have it so that two legs go to the front with one leg near me. I also slightly angle the stick so that it leans toward me, which means I can ever so slightly lean into the support and it is less likely that the stick will topple forward, so it is more stable and provides a better support. You can rest a PCP airgun directly onto the stick and shoot because there is no real recoil, but do not do this with a springer because it will jump if unsupported. Rest the back of your forehand on the stick and support the end of the gun stock in your cupped hand to help control the recoil.

The soaking ground during winter rabbit shooting. Not a great idea to lie on your belly to take shots from a bipod. A shooting stick makes more sense in this scenario.

HUNTING: EQUIPMENT   5

SHOOTING SEATS

Ambushing vermin and setting up ambush positions is a big part of hunting with airguns. This often requires putting oneself in a place and waiting for long periods of time, so it's more practical if the hunter is also as comfortable as possible. Sitting on the floor, assuming it is clean and not waterlogged, or on low-lying tree branches is all very well, but sometimes they are not available or suitable, so a proper shooting seat is useful in such scenarios. Around farm buildings you can use what is available; things like old tyres, drum containers, wooden pallets and so on, make good seats, but they won't be in the middle of the forest or out in the fields.

These days, it is quite common to carry a handy portable seat with you and some come fitted with bags or containers for culled animals, and so combine two functions. There are many different styles, from rucksacks with folding legs, to 'bucket seats', which are ostensibly a small plastic bin with a padded seat on top, covered in camo

A bucket seat that also doubles up as a quarry container, and shooting stick, all prepared and ready for a squirrel shoot.

material, but they all work and do the job. A shooting seat and quarry container might not seem an obvious choice as a piece of essential kit, but all I would say is, go stand in the deep forest for three hours waiting for grey squirrels, and then see how welcome a seat is – or try carrying four flea-ridden rabbits for two miles back to the car, to see how handy a container can be!

RUCKSACKS AND BACKPACKS

Rucksacks are also an essential item. Known affectionately as a 'rucky', they are invaluable, and really useful for simply loading up with all your essentials and taking off to go shooting. You should be able to load most if not all of your paraphernalia into a rucksack, and even if you are leaving it in the boot of your car, they are still very handy for keeping everything secure and in one place. Personally, I prefer one made of a hard-wearing, quiet, weatherproof material, with plenty of external pockets for ease of access in the field, and they don't need to be huge to be effective storage devices.

My current rucksack is a Napier Ranger 5, which is very well made, meets all the criteria, and I can pack all my camouflage clothing into it, together with a camo net, my knives and sharpeners, a flask of water and coffee, pellets, rangefinder, toilet paper, and some general use paraphernalia.

On occasion, rucksacks can be used as a kind of make-shift rest or bipod for your PCP airgun when taking rabbit shots, which will also help to conceal the shooter because they will be positioned lying down behind it. It's often a good idea to lie on your belly in the prone position, with the rucky in front of you, gun rested on top and a camo leaf-net draped over you. This can be very effective, even in the middle of a field with no immediate cover – but stay low! Some hunters use their kit-carrying rucksacks to carry dead quarry, too, and that's fine, but these days there are quarry carriers specifically designed for the job. I prefer to have a rucksack for my kit, materials and consumables, and carry my quarry in something else so that my kit and bag remain clean inside. My portable shooting seat doubles-up as a quarry container, so I don't use the rucksack for this purpose. Dead animals also start smelling after a while, so it's best to delegate the quarry carrying duties to another product.

HUNTING: EQUIPMENT   5

LASER RANGEFINDERS

Estimating distance is very important for hunting. All hunters need to be able to estimate distance accurately. It might well be the case that distance is more of an issue for the .22 calibre – and even more so for the .25 calibre – but it is not unimportant for the .177. Over recent years, the use of laser rangefinders has become more common with airgunners because they obviously remove a lot of the guesswork in distance estimation. Although a rangefinder is a really useful tool, I would say hunters should still try to learn to estimate distance visually – in other words, do not ignore developing this skill.

Rangefinders are not just for estimating the distance of the quarry from the shooter directly, but can be used to estimate the distance of various mid-points of cover between the shooter and quarry, so that the distance that one needs to get to before taking a shot can be calculated before the stalk begins. Using it this way means that as long as the quarry have not moved, you do not have to keep getting the rangefinder out as you stalk toward the animal. You simply need to get to the place you've previous lasered and know to be a suitable distance from the quarry. Hand-held units are most common and good-quality units with lots of features are reasonably priced. Some models of laser rangefinder can be mounted to telescopic sights, which can work in the day and complement night-vision set-ups because rangefinding in the dark can be difficult. These versions can be adjusted to laser the distances on which you place your scope crosshair.

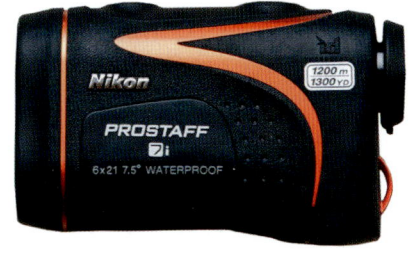

A hand-held laser rangefinder can be an invaluable tool in the field even for the most experienced hunter.

LAMPING KITS AND NIGHT VISION

In the good old days, lamping required a heavy, acid-based battery – an old car or motorbike battery – in a rucksack, long wires running from said battery to a car spotlight, and a mate to hold it all while you did the shooting. Thankfully, things have changed.

5 THE AIRGUNNER'S COMPANION

These days I use a LEDRAY Tactical lamp, which is basically the size of a Cuban cigar and sits on top of the scope. The batteries can be recharged easily and without drama. It is very small and the beam, about 180 metres, is more than bright enough for me. It comes with three small filters, but I've never really used them that much on this unit, to be honest. It is hard not to be successful with systems like this. They do not alter the balance of the gun, are clean and rugged, a joy to use, and of all the hunting methods, lamping is one of the most rewarding. Get a system that is rugged, self-contained, compact, and waterproof.

Night vision (NV) has been a big development, and more and more hunters are opting for an NV set-up on their guns. The big advantage is that the quarry has no idea you are there – no lamp is turned on or off – and in many ways, NV is something of a game changer. You are the ultimate assassin. The downside is primarily one of

Modern lamping units are highly effective and compact. This LEDRAY system gives a 180m beam, three light intensity settings and comes with light filters and scope mounts for 25mm and 30mm tubed scopes.

HUNTING: EQUIPMENT

expense – although many hunters are now making their own systems for a fraction of the price of units from manufacturers. If night shooting is going to be a big part of your hunting, i.e., rats and rabbits, then going down the NV path is a good idea and would appear to be a worthwhile investment. The decision is yours and both methods have their place.

THERMAL SPOTTERS

Thermal spotters are becoming increasingly popular – although their designs for hunting are still in their infancy. These devices allow you to locate hard-to-see quarry by displaying their heat signature. The units available are expensive, but can be extremely helpful for certain situations – woodland shooting, for example – and for certain airgun species such as grey squirrels. At the time of writing, the Pulsar units appear to offer the best balance between cost, function, and usefulness. They start at around £1300, but if you are going to be involved in some serious grey squirrel shooting, this might be a worthwhile investment.

CAMOUFLAGE AND HUNTING APPAREL

Surprisingly, the need and use of camouflage is debated within the hunting community and so it is perhaps important to give this topic some discussion. Many people make the claim that they can shoot rabbits and other quarry in little more than a T-shirt and shorts, so there is no real need for much camouflage. However, this is a fallacious argument against the use of camouflage and the concept of concealment, reflecting a serious misunderstanding. People who argue against its use have no way of knowing how much better they could have been if they had used it. Humans also have selective memories – we remember all the vermin we shoot more than all the ones we totally missed, or spooked along the way. A hunter might well have brought 20 rabbits home, but spooked 60 of them in the process. Camouflage, had it been used, might have improved that ratio significantly.

The argument against the use of camouflage is over-played, and those making it misunderstand the real issue, which I will attempt to describe below. I also find that people who are a little 'anti-camouflage' tend to shoot FAC rifles or FAC airguns, meaning that you do not need to get anywhere near as close to the quarry in the first place, and use lamping as a method most of the time on things like rabbits and foxes, or shoot mainly from inside a 4x4 Jeep. These experiences taint their view or bias their memory of hunting with 12 ft.lbs. airguns in non-lamping situations. I also find the arguments surrounding camouflage get confounded and conflated with the concept of concealment. The truth is, one can certainly be concealed without camouflage, but camouflage can provide superior concealment.

Now, when I started hunting, I simply could not afford camouflage clothing. At this time, I simply wore dark clothes like black, navy, and dark green tops, and jeans. Did I manage to shoot anything? Of course, I did. Did it give a degree of concealment? Yes, it provided me with a certain level of proficiency, but these clothes were not the most functional, not the quietest, and were not made with the hunter in mind. They were far from waterproof or windproof, not the warmest in winter, and worked better in an ambush situation rather than for stalking. They also worked better on some quarry – rabbits – than others – woodpigeons or crows. So the real issue is not whether you can shoot without camo clothing – of course, you can – but whether everyday clothing provides you with optimal concealment and proficiency in the field and, to my mind, the answer is clear 'no'.

It is the case that some animal species have poorer eyesight than others, or than we humans. Rabbits are often a good example, although it is not entirely accurate to say they have bad eyesight. I've shot many whilst I was wearing just dark clothes, sticking to the shadows or perimeter hedgerow and slowly encroaching on them, or waiting in ambush as they run to me, but I've shot more, and got closer with camouflage than I ever have without it. So the issue is this: Camouflage is not necessary for shooting some quarry species, but it is helpful, and I am not aware of any situation where it makes things worse – not one.

There are other factors to consider. Some pest/vermin species might be very used to being shot at, and they can be particularly skittish. Woodpigeon and crows spring to mind here; there is no way you are getting close to them showing lots of skin, particularly your face or hands, or wearing bright clothes, unless they are used to having humans around and perceive no threat. These scenarios are very unlike those where people drive around golf courses at night, lamping semi-tame rabbits from a 4x4 Jeep. Firstly, in this situation the rabbits are not overly fussed by the presence of humans, and secondly, if you're behind a lamp you could wear a wedding dress and still bag plenty! So these situations are not comparable; one situation cannot be used

HUNTING: EQUIPMENT

as an argument against the need for camouflage in the other situation. It all depends on context, what you are shooting, when and how. However, I personally recommend to those serious about hunting with airguns, to obtain their own hunting apparel and for camouflage clothing to be part of that. One certainly does not need to go mad and pay the highest prices for the latest stuff, but effective hunters are concealed hunters and a modest investment should be made.

The job of camouflage is to aid concealment. In terms of visual concealment, the pattern is designed specifically to break up the outline of the human body, allowing the hunter to blend into the background, and the more effective it is at doing it, the better. Although other general field clothing can certainly help with concealment, camouflage is the most effective at breaking up the human shape. As a camouflage pattern, basic British army patterns (DPM patterns) are perfectly suited, effective, and very cheap – absolutely up to the job, no question. They have been the standard for decades and there is no reason to assume that they will not go on being just as effective. These garments provide very good concealment, but the garments many ex-army stores sell are arguably not as fully rounded as some of the more recently developed hunting apparel. So, the reasons for going for something slightly more expensive might not just be about visual concealment, but a broader functionality in the field.

The more expensive ranges of clothing often have membranes in them, which are very effective at protecting you from the harsh elements in a way that a basic ex-army service jacket rarely will. They also tend to contain more pockets, of different sizes, for a variety of functions in the field, and the material can be quieter than standard army issue apparel.

These days, modern hunting apparel often has high definition, 3D-imaging print like the Realtree range, (i.e., Advantage Timber, Hardwoods Green, Realtree Xtra, Realtree Xtra Green, APG) or the Mossy Oak range. It is debatable whether or not these are any more effective in concealment relative to standard army-surplus patterns, but the broader functionality of modern clothing has advanced in recent years. It's not just about the colours used because some quarry will not have the same colour receptors in their eyes or brains that we humans do, but it is also about how these patterns break up your shape and movement. In a later section I will discuss the importance of something known as 'biological motion' and how camouflage can help with hiding these signals from animals that are hard-wired to flee when they perceive it.

THE AIRGUNNER'S COMPANION

Another form of concealment is noise. The fabric needs to be quiet, snag free, devoid of rattling metal zip, fastening noises and of that high-pitched rustle, from which cheaper garments suffer a great deal. Many years ago, I purchased a jacket and trousers with the Realtree Hardwoods Green pattern – it was a chance purchase, and I've been unable to locate the same manufacturer in shops ever since. They are made from an extremely quiet material – one of the best I've noticed on any hunting apparel; they allow for very quiet stalking through brambles and bushes and they don't snag when you brush up against dense foliage. Fabulous!

One suggestion I'd make is to never purchase your camouflage without looking at it in person. You need to know the material is quiet and well made. Some of the most popular brands in the hunting media can produce some of the most useless garments when evaluated for quietness. On the whole, items I have purchased from Seeland, Harkila, Deerhunter, Napier, and Garlands have been of far superior quality to anything I've seen from cheaper manufacturers in the UK aimed at the mass budget market. The quietness these more expensive items give you in the field is worth its weight in gold, and they will last for years, paying for themselves over and over.

On the whole, camouflage clothing – jacket, trousers, gloves, hat, balaclava, snood, face mesh, and so on – is more than sufficient if used effectively, but many hunters take things even further, either by covering themselves and their gun in camo-netting or using a ghillie suit with a loose-leaf covering to help break up the human shape. To the human eye, these methods work well in terms of aiding concealment, and if you have the resources and motivation to explore such methods – go for it! Don't let others put you off; explore these items for yourself and how you might make them work for the shooting you do. Concealment is a relative thing and there will be a theoretical point at which your concealment is sufficient, and additional attempts redundant. Some might say that being almost invisible is always the 'optimal' solution and so we should all seek to achieve absolute excellence at this. Indeed, but it is not always practical or obtainable on every hunting foray, and some compromise is nearly always more realistic.

I can personally vouch for the protection that membrane-equipped clothing can provide against the elements. I remember going on a five-day shooting foray when the intention was to hit the grey squirrels very hard. It rained every day, and on two days it was absolutely torrential, with strong winds. I got caught out in the woods on the first day when the weather moved in and my outer clothing ended up being wetter than a fish's wet bits! It was bloody awful, but when I returned home and removed the outerwear, I was completely dry underneath. You might feel silly in camo gear at times, but it has a job to do and it is important that it does it well. Could I hunt in a wax jacket and jeans? Yes, of course I could. Would I be as comfortable, and have the functionality, quietness, warmth and dryness that I get from the other more comprehensive gear I have? I reckon, almost certainly not.

One final word on modern hunting apparel and the weather membranes many of them contain. Whilst these can be fantastic at protecting you from the elements in the depths of winter, your body also needs to be able to breathe, particularly if you're going off on a long stalk. So check items for being 'breathable' as well as giving protection. Some thought to what you wear underneath your exterior camo gear can help to cope here, but on the whole you don't want a 'boil-in-the-bag' situation from your jacket and trousers combo. It can be a good idea to have a summer and winter set-up, perhaps the main difference being the base layers that you wear underneath.

At the moment, my camo gear consists of mainly the Realtree patterns (Hardwoods Green, Advantage Timber, APG and standard BPM patterns) from some of the manufacturers listed above. These are effective throughout the year for hunting in fields and woodlands, and I find the colours and contrast well suited to the varied UK countryside. They are also hard-wearing and I can kneel in a puddle and not feel wet, because of their weather-proofing. Depending on the season and weather, I can wear thermal undergarments or just jeans and a T-shirt underneath, but due to how well they protect against the elements, there is no need for anything excessive underneath. I tend to keep my hunting underclothes thin and versatile to counteract the job the outer wear has to do. This makes the clothes bearable – warm when you are out in the cold, but not too warm if you are engaged in some physical exertion or on a hot day.

Camouflage works, but it does not make you invisible. It has its role to play and you need to know how to get the most from it. While dressing up to resemble Arnold Schwarzenegger in films like *Predator* and *Commando* is unnecessary, and a somewhat hilarious thought, concealment by camouflage has its place. Pick a good visual camouflage pattern, made of hard-wearing, low-sound material that is waterproof and fitted with an abundance of pockets and features. You need to invest, but there is no need to go out and buy the most expensive stuff. Some jackets I've seen can cost £600, which is just silly, expensive and certainly out of my price bracket, but there are some bargains to be had – and not at the cost of functionality in the field. Again I'd say, 'buy cheap buy twice'.

Mixing and matching camouflage with other primary-coloured clothes is also effective – you don't always need to be draped completely in the stuff to benefit from it. A camouflage jacket coupled with gloves, face-covering, a hat and dark olive green field trousers is perfectively fine for many circumstances. If I sit still in the hedgerow, woods, or behind a camo-leaf netted hide, squirrels and rabbits rarely notice me when I'm wearing such combinations. You might even get away with some stalking in the right light, but the level of concealment, whilst good for many species, will be reduced for others. Harkila make some wonderful, general-purpose field trousers made from very functional material; fully waterproof, snag free, and with lots of useful pockets. I have a pair of their 'Pro Hunter X' trousers and can recommend them for their durability and functionality in the field. These are not camouflaged, but can be coupled to camouflage and used effectively.

FOOTWEAR

Leave the cheap wellies at home – they have poor soles, no ankle support and are loud as they slap about when you walk. In the summer, the humble, dark coloured trainer is fine, but limited. The summer can also be pretty wet at times in the UK and certain types of land can hold moisture for days, often meaning that it rarely dries out. For me, my general footwear would be the sort of fell-walking, waterproof-type boot or shoe. You might be walking great distances as part of your hunting forays, and you will be thankful for a comfortable boot that has been designed to be effective under such conditions. As well as providing excellent foot and ankle support, these are warm, quiet, and typically 100% waterproof. They have internal soles for comfort, and excellent foot tread giving good stability across a variety of surfaces. Modern designs also mean that such footwear can be very quiet as well, and you can stalk just as effectively in them as you can in soft trainers. These features are essential for hunting in the weather conditions the UK throws at us. A good pair might be expensive – around £100–£160 on average – but will last years and cope with everything you can throw at them. On a personal note, walking boots or walking shoes are also important for my hunting, due to the challenging terrain of the Lake District. I've taken shots whilst standing in shallow but fast-flowing streams, and been completely dry when wearing this type of footwear. Other options might include stalking boots for shooting around farm buildings and less demanding ground.

HUNTING: EQUIPMENT

CAMO-NETTING AND HIDES

Adding coverage to aid concealment is a neat trick. Camo-netting is very useful and highly versatile in this regard. You can mount the netting on poles, or indeed, just drape it on yourself sitting there in the hedgerow or woodland. There are a few main types including; those of a fine, smooth-mesh netting with a camouflage print on it that you shoot over; one that is just a coarse and dense fabric net, and another which is a coarse net but with fake leaves overlaid on it, known as 'leaf-netting'. My personal preference is for the latter two, with coarse-cut material or leaf netting because they have the capacity to provide a greater break-up of the human shape, and I can place my gun barrel through the large holes in the net, allowing me to remain concealed behind it as opposed to having to shoot over it.

Netting can be used in a variety of ways; as a simple portable blind or screen erected between hunter and quarry; draped on the hunter sitting in the hedge, or lying on the ground – acting now like a kind of ghillie suit – or used to build a full impromptu hide. The aim is to provide cover, when little or none is present – you are adding to what nature has provided, or not, as the case may be. Due to its versatility, camo-netting can be used to help shoot a variety of quarry and can be coupled to other techniques like decoying for shooting corvids and woodpigeons, assuming that you have enough of it to build a decent hide. Adding naturally available materials like leaves, twigs, mossy grass and threading branches throught it will help to make it appear more realistic, providing even more concealment, and is worth it if you are going to leave the netting up in a fixed place for a while. Netting can be used effectively in all shooting scenarios from shooting in woodland to wide open fields and so its versatility is excellent. I tend to own a few sizes of netting for different purposes. For example, I have netting I use for hide building that is quite large to ensure a lot of coverage. Something like 6m x 2.5m would be standard with this aim in mind, but smaller 'off-cuts' are ideal for just draping on yourself whilst you simply sit in an unprepared ambush location, the gorse bushes, or even out in the field. I've heard it said by some that they dislike some camo-leaf netting as it can be made from a material that rustles a lot. This can be the case, but I've used various materials over the years and the rabbits, squirrels, and woodpigeon don't seem to mind.

There are now also a number of commercially available, pre-built, pop-up hides. They come in various designs, but the aim is the same – concealment when the coverage is not optimal. Hides are great things and they can be made from scratch, the old-fashioned way, using branches, twigs, leaves, and the cover available in the woodland. Make sure you get permission from the landowner first before building one, though! There is a real fieldcraft to building your own real hide manually, and part of me feels like it's an important skill for all hunters to have. However, the downside is that they take a lot of time to build and maintain, and any green foliage will eventually die off. Portable, pop-up hides are more convenient because they can be set up quickly and can be moved around easily. Some hunters add real materials to the pop-up hide, to improve its effect by making it look even more natural. This natural material comes in the form of fallen branches, twigs, etc., although man-made camo-leaf netting can also be added to great effect. Pop-up hides are fine for shooting grey squirrels and rabbits, but corvids will tend to require more convincing. I'd recommend keeping things as natural as possible for these canny creatures.

Creating these spaces of optimised concealment only helps to aid your success at shooting all species. There is also plenty of space in here and a good view of the surrounding fields. With a flask of coffee and a ploughman's sandwich it's a nice place to spend a few hours.

HUNTING: EQUIPMENT

Hides are typically associated with bird shooting and their heritage is perhaps more with shotgun shooting, but these methods are now firmly established in airgunning and we have learned a great deal from our shotgun brothers and sisters over the years. There is no reason why hide shooting cannot be used by the airgunner to shoot many of the same pest bird species as those targeted by shotgunners – woodpigeons, crows, rooks – even more so when coupled with methods like decoying. When utilised properly, natural hides, leaf netting and pop-up hides can be an extremely effective approach for aiding concealment during hunting.

Placing or building the hide in woodland and integrating it well with its surroundings will nearly always lead to success, but out in open fields things become more difficult. The real trick is to pick a good location, and the information you use to inform your decision will obviously vary depending on the quarry being targeted. Again, it is a case of doing your prior research. Deciding where to put your hide is the same as deciding on the location of any of your favourite ambush positions, only now, you require even more concealment. Try to ensure a solid backdrop and good front field of view, with suitable concealment and make sure you are set up in range of your expected quarry, but not too close. When establishing a hide, it is important not to be seen in it, even when not shooting from it. Animals will soon associate your presence with it if you are seen there, and bird species especially will completely vacate the area if needs be.

WILDLIFE, TRAIL AND SURVEILLANCE CAMERAS

OK, to be honest, they're not an essential piece of kit, per se, but digital wildlife cameras can be a very effective research tool for the hunter, particularly if there are many acres of land to cover. The camera types are wide and varied, but typically contain memory cards that can be viewed on a laptop, and other more expensive versions can be accessed via mobile phones and laptops. Depending on the make and model, you can capture still images, take short movie clips, or both. Ideally, they need to be set to be triggered by movement and for the images to be time-stamped and contain whatever data required to help the hunter establish patterns with some precision. In a later section, I discuss how they can be used in conjunction with squirrel feeders to ascertain the squirrel feeding times. This is very helpful when trying to cover vast woodland and a large squirrel problem. Wildlife cams are just one example of the high-tech nature of modern-day hunting with air rifles. Prices vary and my advice is not to go too cheaply. I currently use units made by Browning, which represent a nice trade-off between function, durability, build quality and price. I also hear good things about the Bushnell and SpyPoint brands.

DECOYS (DEEKS)

Decoying, in the sense of just using decoys and not carrion and decoys, is the one hunting method I probably do the least, probably because for most of my hunting life I've had shooting permissions for lots of forest and woodland, where I prefer to ambush the sitty trees of woodpigeons or the lookout trees of corvids. The woodland

A collection of my flocked corvid decoys including magpies, crows and crow magnums. The flocked coating really aids with realism, particularly in harsh sunlight when plastic coating can look overly shiny and artificial. Couple these deeks to an opened up squirrel or rabbit and you could be in for a good day's shooting.

HUNTING: EQUIPMENT

provides me with plenty of natural opportunity to hit the quarry without much additional need for decoying. However, I do like to complement things from time to time, and mix things up a little with a spot of corvid decoying, mixed with fresh carrion. Most serious hunters will have a set of decoys (deeks) and they can be put to very effective use. I'd recommend purchasing 'flocked' deeks, if possible. 'Flocking' simply means that the decoy is covered in a fuzzy material, giving it a more realistic look and texture that doesn't reflect the light in the way cheaper, plastic, shiny ones do. They are worth the few quid more. Deeks can be used either on their own or with an opened up squirrel or rabbit, or some eggs – which can be very effective. I find putting a magpie deek on a fence post whilst having an opened up rabbit or grey squirrel carcass on the ground is a really good way to attract real magpies into range.

A BIG FREEZER

Seriously ... think about it. Where are you going to put all those bunnies and woodpigeons?

MISCELLANEOUS ITEMS

The list covered above should not be considered comprehensive. In addition to the items required for looking after and maintaining your airgun there are many other important items, including; disposable rubber gloves and disinfectant, wire cutters, a small axe or Kukri and a pair of secateurs. For very general needs I also carry a selection of plastic wire ties, paracord of various thicknesses and lengths, and small metal fixings like karabiners or variations of them. These can all be used to help with setting up hides, netting, or the general manipulation of your local environment. Many farmers are very appreciative of the odd gate being given some form of attention with temporary fixings should they require it. In the past, I've tied up fallen iron gates, created make-shift cord hinges or new loops for securing the gate into its closed position. This not only helps me because I can enter and leave spaces more easily, but I also feel this is just generally a very respectful thing to do for the landowner, who trusts you, and it represents a way of saying 'thank you' to them.

5 THE AIRGUNNER'S COMPANION

General miscellaneous items for airgun maintenance. Having invested in an airgun you need to look after it. Even if you do not strip or tune your own gun it is important to have some basic tools so you can check everything is secure and you always need products for keeping the woodwork and metalwork looking its best. Look after your airgun and it will look after you. Never underestimate the importance of the oily rag!

If you are going to be out in the field for a period of time, it is essential to take some form of food, and bottles of water or a flask of coffee or tea. You can get tired quickly in the field and you always want to ensure that you are safe and have the energy to get back to the car safely. If I'm not travelling far, then I will leave of lot of this in the car and pop back to it from time to time, but if I'm trekking for a while over the land I'll take what I can with me in my rucky. A first-aid kit containing the basics – plasters, bandages, antiseptic creams, wipes and so on – is also useful. If you are taking daily medication, don't forget to take it on the day or take it with you in case you stay out longer than intended, which can happen if the shooting is good. Finally, if shooting in very remote places, make sure someone knows where you are going and when to expect you back.

6 Hunting: Fieldcraft

THE IMPORTANCE OF FIELDCRAFT

Fieldcraft is integral to all aspects of hunting. It is a collection of real skills and makes the difference between a proficient hunter and a really poor one. The hunter with the most expensive gun, equipped with all the latest toys and wearing the latest camouflage will not necessarily come home with the biggest bag of culled pests. My money will always be on the hunter with the most developed fieldcraft skills, although they also might have the latest toys and gizmos, of course! Fieldcraft requires a comprehensive understanding of wildlife and nature as well as shooting and hunting methods.

Fieldcraft is not something we ever truly master. It is something we are constantly learning, it is an ever-moving target because the wildlife and countryside is an ever-flowing source of information, which the receptive hunter will seek to observe. It is a vast subject that deserves a book all of its own. Even 'old dogs' of hunting will not know it all. When it all comes together in the field it is very rewarding, and when it all goes wrong, there is still plenty to learn from the experience. If you are a beginner to hunting, do not be intimidated by the amount of information that you need to learn. Take one step at a time, relish the challenge and your exploits will be more rewarding in the long run. The important thing is to learn from every hunting foray.

OBSERVATION

Arguably one of the most important, yet neglected, aspects of fieldcraft is to go out on to your shoots and observe the behaviour of your intended quarry without the intention to shoot it just yet. Prior research is key here. In this sense, you're not just researching the land and the challenges it poses, but the behaviour of the animals you intend to shoot. To ensure that you are truly going to observe and not get side-tracked and seduced into premature shooting, do not take your gun when out observing animal behaviour. A good pair of binoculars and an open, observant mind are all that is needed.

To illustrate what I mean, consider a rabbit-shooting scenario. Go out the first time, keep your distance so as not to alert any bunny of your presence and simply observe them; locate the warrens and the runs; look for the scratches in the earth, and the droppings, and discern from where they tend to emerge. Rabbits often find their way around by smell, particularly at night, so knowing where the runs are, or the bare scratched patches of earth full of droppings will tell you where they frequent and feed the most – and even where to lamp. It is often just a case of joining up the dots!

Try to get a feel for how far out from the warrens the rabbits are going, based on your assessment of the signs on the ground, and watching them when they are out feeding and running about. Look for juvenile behaviour, running and playing for fun, or the sign of old bucks – bits missing from ears due to prior fighting often signals an older buck. Look for plump-looking does that might be pregnant. How confident or skittish do they appear to be? What times do they seem to be out and about? What about the presence of other predators, such as foxes or buzzards? Try to get a feel for the localised ecology as best you can in an attempt to get a feel for how to hit them best. Rabbits tend to like nice weather and can often be found on

Observation time. I'm interested in watching the bunnies, woodpigeon and collared doves in this extensive woodland. Find a shaded or relatively hidden location that provides a good view, and simply watch the behaviour of the animals around you. Keep your distance. Where are the rabbits emerging from? Where do they prefer to feed? How many are there? Basically, ask yourself what is happening here and why. Leave the gun at home or in the car during these initial observation sessions.

HUNTING: FIELDCRAFT

the warm side of the terrain, so use this knowledge to inform your observations and ultimately, hunting strategy.

Consider shooting woodpigeons. Again, find a place where you are hidden from their view and observe them flying into and out of fields. Note the times, numbers and direction of entry, landing positions etc. Observe their feeding opportunities in the field and, if possible, their 'sitty' trees where they like to rest and observe in between feeding times. Are you planning to hit the sitty trees or decoy them to the ground near your yet-to-be-built hide? Watching what they are doing, asking yourself why they are there, and thinking about how best to hit them is all part of the same process of prior research. Although you can often walk around, get lucky and bag a few, a truly successful hunter is an informed hunter. Importantly, you need to do this for every shooting location you have because the animal behaviour will be different in different places.

Hunting wild rabbits in remote woodlands or fields, where there are many predators and they see few humans, is very different to shooting rabbits on a golf course where Mr Ponsonby-Frobisher-Smyth is on the putting green in dodgy tartan trousers, some 15 yards from a bunch of bunnies tucking undisturbed into their easy pickings. Some aspects of animal behaviour might be constant, but a lot of it has adapted to its immediate surroundings and so animal behaviour will vary due to context, and what it knows or has come to know. So, doing an excellent job of recognisance in one location does not mean you do not need to do it again elsewhere – you most certainly need to do it, and do so constantly. Carrying out such prior research will almost inevitably lead to increased success if you observe and apply that knowledge correctly. The principles outlined here will be applicable to all quarry species – even the humble rat will leave signs of his existence for you to explore and plan your ambush accordingly.

HOW TO USE YOUR CAMOUFLAGE AND ENVIRONMENT EFFECTIVELY

You are far from invisible simply by wearing camouflage. Indeed, camouflage is not necessarily something you wear, it's something you use. Camouflage clothing is important for concealing your presence. Being hidden or camouflaged does not happen automatically. It requires some effort on your part to optimise the effect

THE AIRGUNNER'S COMPANION

and get the most out of it. The hunter needs an awareness of themselves and their surroundings at all times. They need to be able to appreciate how they appear, from the viewpoint of the animal being targeted. This is a skill known in human psychology as 'perspective-taking', a kind of mental spatial rotation so that you can imagine how you appear from the animal's perspective, looking back toward yourself.

A good exercise here is to imagine yourself standing in the middle of a flat field, with a rabbit 20 yards in front of you. Imagine there is nothing behind you to blend with, just the large flat field and a clear blue sky. Now, from the perspective of the rabbit, which is also low down on the ground, your silhouette will be clearly marked against the sky and you'll stick out like a sore thumb. Remember, the rabbits view is from a low vantage point, on the ground, and the angle between the rabbit and you (low rabbit + high human) means that the rabbit will see your outline elevated against the sky, which provides no cover whatsoever. Having an awareness about these relationships is the process of perspective-taking and is vital for optimal effectiveness in the field. Stealth is not just about hiding behind something, but also having an awareness of your total surroundings and how to use them to best effect.

Using the environment effectively will invariably mean wearing camouflage clothing, or something similar to assist with concealment. For some species, like rabbits, camouflage might be less important, but more so for other species like crows and woodpigeon. However, you never know what you will encounter while out and about, so some attempt to conceal oneself will always lead to more success than failure. It's best to be over-prepared than get caught short in the field. The woodpigeon won't wait while you go home to change!

If ambushing, then it is important to ensure the forward view from the perspective of the hunter is as wide and clear as can be, whilst ensuring that the actual hunter's position is as concealed as possible. Good concealment includes the hunter having a dense and rich coverage behind them – known as a backdrop – to facilitate good blending, and, if possible, also some coverage in front of them. This is where camo-netting and hides can be particularly effective. If the use of such apparatus is not possible, then use what is readily available to best effect. Imagine playing hide and seek. Now, just by scanning the environment, where do the best hiding spots appear to be? Do these also provide a good ambush shooting position? Look for dense foliage and try to place yourself in the middle of it whilst ensuring that nothing hampers your pellet on the way to the intended shooting space. Look for sections where the light is either 'broken up', perhaps via the overhanging tree canopy, or the presence of shadows – these make good ambush points in which to place yourself. In fact, shadows and shade are things always to be looking for because these are good friends to the hunter.

The perimeter tree line from a section of woodland. Note the provision of mixed lighting and the abundance of shaded areas around the tree line. Learn to use these to your advantage. This is where to build your hide and place yourself when targeting quarry that are out in the fields and towards the direction of the camera here. Make sure you remain located in the dark recesses behind the tree line.

I am of the opinion that hiding the bright flesh of the face and hands can be more important at close range than the need for camo trousers versus dark pants. Animals understand the configuration of faces, and those of possible predators. A camouflage hat, balaclava, snood, or face-net are all good options for masking the face and basic gloves for the hands. The woodland provides many natural opportunities for effectively using camouflage to give the hunter an edge. Fallen and split trees can provide something to hide behind, something to rest the gun on, and something to sit in front of and use as a backdrop to help fracture your outline. Dense brambles, long grass, tree bark … can all be used to great effect. In the open field, use hedgerows and the shadows they project on a sunny day or evening. When trying to get the most out of camouflage, think in three dimensions and ask yourself, am I covered from behind and in front of me? The more you remain still, the better. Good camouflage will help to break up your outline, but too many sudden movements and it can become really easy to spot the human shape. Keep movements to a minimum and keep them slow and fluid. This applies not just to situations when you are shouldering the gun, but all head movements while simply waiting in ambush as well. Keep still and be patient.

In studies of human vision, there is a phenomenon known as 'biological motion'. Imagine a human wearing a black leotard with some glow-in-the-dark markers (small white balls) dotted over their body, down their arms, legs, across the chest and shoulders. Now imagine that person standing amongst a whole collection of other glow-in-the-dark markers that are not attached to them, but just suspended in the room. With all the lights turned off, and using special cameras, the person is invisible and all you see is a meaningless collection of random static marker dots. However, as soon as the individual moves – say, just walking across the room – they are almost instantly recognisable as being 'alive' and the whole human body shape, swinging arms, legs, torso, direction of motion, becomes cued, implied, and difficult not to see. In other words, the perception of a living moving human body is strongly cued, even though all the brain actually sees is a collection of dots moving in a certain coordinated way. Some studies have shown you can even tell, based on biological motion alone, if the person is male or female, young or old, and even if walking with a limp.

Animals (prey) are very good at inferring the presence of predators from this type of biological motion. In other words, they can tell, with a very starved and minimal amount of visual information, that something 'alive' is moving, and its basic shape. This is why, when wearing camouflage the hunter needs to keep movements slow and fluid so as not to cue, via biological motion, the presence of a coordinated shape – a human – breaking away from its background and surroundings. Sharp changes in motion will trigger the awareness in the animal and make them alert to your presence. Even a sudden head or neck movement can be sufficient to trigger the implied perception of your whole body. Such movement is all the animal needs to spook it and make it take immediate evasive survival action. I personally believe this is a much stronger trigger in animals than actual visual acuity. A rabbit does not need to know 'what' it is that is moving, just that something big is moving and it is likely to be a predator.

HUNTING: FIELDCRAFT 6

Hunting in the harsh sunlight of a midwinter day. Low, bright sunlight can cause problems for concealment when out in the open because your movement will be easy to see and you will cast long shadows which also move in sympathy with you. Assuming it's winter and you have no camo-netting in place, one way to counter this is to use your environment to optimal effect by placing yourself in the shade, or areas where light and shade are heavily intermixed.

TOP RIGHT AND ABOVE RIGHT: *An area of mixed lighting can help to break up the human shape.* RIGHT: *Again using a shaded area, but also hiding behind a fallen tree helps to provide additional coverage from the perspective of the quarry. Note also, the fast moving stream provides background sounds that can mask the noise you might make when on the move, so you can get closer.*

TOP LEFT: *A crucial aspect of concealment is to optimise one's immediate environment. Here, I simply placed myself inside a shaded clearing under a large rhododendron bush. Providing the hunter stays reasonably still, this level of concealment is more than sufficient for the unsuspecting rabbit or squirrel. Improving the backdrop, or kneeling down would elevate the effect even further..*

LEFT: *Make sure you can see while not being seen. Staying close to prominent natural features, like this conifer tree, helps to optimise concealment and place you in the shade, whilst giving you a good view of your surroundings.*

BOTTOM LEFT: *Using the local environment to help break up the human shape. To the human eye, I might be easy to see here in the winter woodland, but to the rabbit or grey squirrel, which has no conception of the airgun, I will appear to them as part of the tree – providing I don't give any motion cues to signal the presence of something 'alive'. You do not always need to be absolutely invisible to the human eye, to be invisible to the animal eye. The really crucial thing is to have no motion cues and have your human shape intermixed and broken up with your surroundings.*

HUNTING: FIELDCRAFT 6

TOP RIGHT: *Even in the stark winter months, the hunter can still have sufficient foliage with which to blend and help to break up their outline. Providing no major movements are made, this level of concealment is more than sufficient for most quarry species. The environment could be optimised more by the addition of some hide work or camo-leaf netting.*

RIGHT: *A demanding one this because there is no foliage to use at all. So what to do? Here I'm trying to merge with the mossy dry-stone wall. Again, using 'perspective-taking', the only thing the quarry will see, from its perspective looking down on me, is my head and the end of my moderator and scope. The rest of me is concealed from its perspective. However, if grouped strongly to the wall, I will just appear, from that perspective, as being part of the wall itself, and no threat will be noticed.*

BOTTOM RIGHT: *Ideally, I should be on the other side of the tree for this shot because I shoot right-handed, and going around obstacles like trees or buildings is always best from an anti-clockwise position. However, in this case, there is a 40ft ravine the other side of the tree. So what to do? I stood behind the tree and shouldered the gun so the quarry could not see that action take place – the tree was between us. Then I emerged and stuck close to the tree trunk, in a shooting position and moved slowly until I reached the position in the photo. I used the tree trunk to support my forehand and steady the shot. Again, I'm trying to merge with or 'group to' the tree from the perspective of the quarry (perspective-taking). Only the left-hand side of my body would have been visible to the quarry from the shooting angle.*

This has implications for those that like to add camouflage to their rifle stock, barrel and moderator, with the idea that it aids concealment. It does not. An airgun does not have biological motion – it's an object devoid of its own motion. The hunter moves the airgun –going into the shoulder, for example – but the airgun itself will not be seen as a threat by the quarry, although your body movement will be, if it is seen. This is why I have always been unconvinced by those who go to these efforts – to my mind it's pointless. You have to think like your quarry, not a human. Rabbits, wood and feral pigeons and crows are more than used to seeing bright objects, shiny plastic containers, silage bags, pallets, old tyres, and other objects around the farm, and shimmering moving rivers and streams, or swaying tree branches, and not be spooked by any of it. This is because none of these objects have biological motion.

A photo taken from the perspective of a squirrel feeder. This is what Mr Squirrel 'sees'. If you can, it is often a good idea to have the sunlight shine in their faces, not yours. This also reduces the chances of glare from your gun or optics, if you think that's an issue. However, be careful not to cast shadows right into the kill space. In woodland shooting, the surrounding foliage often helps to break up your own shadow so it's less of an issue than being out in open fields.

HUNTING: FIELDCRAFT

The quarry 'know' that those objects are not 'alive' – in an animal sense – and do not move in the manner of animal-living things.

On a personal note, I know I get my camouflage and concealment right most of the time. One of my shoots is a stately home with extensive grounds, and on summer evenings, members of the public, and residents of the nearby accommodation, go wandering on the footpaths that weave through the woods, sometimes with their dogs in tow. They never see me, not even the dogs. I can be looking right at them and they are all none the wiser. I've been narrowly missed and buzzed by many birds flying through the hedgerows – a bit like King Kong on the Empire State building – I've had brown hares walk right past me, and sat alongside rabbits within 8 yards of my position with them happily feeding.

STALKING

The limit on muzzle energy on legal UK airguns places certain limitations on the hunter. While it is certainly the case that airgun pellets are still carrying enough energy to kill quarry some 50 or 60 yards downrange from the shooter, few of we mortals are precise and consistent enough at those distances – and this is far from humane. Of course, the modern Internet is awash with people claiming excellence at distances far in excess of this. My opinion is that they are either really bad at judging distance, or they read a lot of fiction. The reality is that a lot of the time you will spot your quarry at ranges beyond those that are ideal. Two things can happen in this scenario; either the quarry can come to you – rabbits will often run right toward you – providing you're well-hidden and downwind, or you need to stalk down the quarry to effective ranges.

Stalking requires stealth and is a fundamental hunting skill for airgunners. It requires a quick assessment of the environment and situation and how this can be used to give you, the hunter, an advantage. Stalking, like ambushing, takes time and patience. You are working toward an end point, cutting the distance to an effective range, and the presentation of the optimal shot. It can be both deeply frustrating and highly rewarding.

First things first. Once you've spotted the potential target, assess the situation around you. In which direction is the wind blowing, and assuming it's a sunny evening, where is the sun? If the wind is blowing from behind you, chances are your smell and noise will be transmitted more toward the animal, giving you away much sooner than is helpful. This does not make things impossible, just potentially more challenging. Ideally, you want the wind blowing into your face and away from the quarry. This helps to diffuse sound and odour away from the animal. If the sun is behind you this might mean that your shadow, projecting some way forward on the ground, gives elongated movement cues, possibly toward the animal. Be aware of this because animals might respond to the projected movement from your shadow as a threat, long before they actually spot you. The net consequence of all of this is that the animal is alerted of your presence long before you get into an effective range, so always be aware of your shadow if stalking in sunny weather.

The next thing to think about is where, ideally, you would like to get to in order to take the shot. Perhaps there are a few nice options, perhaps there is only one. Take time to make a decision; estimate the distance of the shot from your chosen position to the animal, and also how much ground you need to cover to get to your destination in order to take the shot. You can do this informally in your head, or better still, use a laser rangefinder before beginning the stalk, and mark where you need to get to. Once decided, now consider the line of approach or route, which will rarely be in a straight line toward the animal – far from it. You might need to consider some convoluted approaches, but ones that give you the best cover and the best shooting opportunity at the end of it. What sort of terrain will you be walking over en route to your chosen spot? Is it dried out leaves and twigs that will crackle a lot when walked upon, or sloppy mud?

You should also give some thought to whether you shoot right- or left-handed, and how to stalk around buildings or obstacles. For example, I shoot with the gun in my right shoulder and so move around buildings in an anti-clockwise direction whenever possible. If I used my left shoulder and did this, I'd need to break cover more and move away from the building or cover more, in order to make the shot. Obviously, if you are left-handed, try to go around things in a clockwise direction.

Now consider all the available cover. Farm buildings, machinery, tractors and trailers, old walls, old tyres, wooden pallets, rubble, trees, bushes, hedges, bales of straw, feeding bags and troughs, and so on, between you and what you are intending to stalk is ideal. If you cannot see the animal at various points en route to it, chances are it cannot see you, although it might still hear and smell you, so move slowly and in a considerate fashion. Use all the available shadows and cover. Don't rush it, pause frequently, look and listen. Move slowly and quietly from point to point. If you must

HUNTING: FIELDCRAFT 6

Having stalked this far, use the stone wall to blend with and provide cover. From the perspective of the bunny 30 yards away, the hunter will be almost invisible up against the wall. Trying to getting much closer, with so little cover available, would be difficult, to say the least, so it is often a good idea to know where it is you intend to get to, before the stalk.

be within sight of the animal, then it is advisable not to look directly at it. At a basic level, wild animals understand threatening postures and being stared at. Walking in the distance, in a direction and manner that does not appear threatening will be more successful as a technique. The trick here is to take a visual scan of the scene, assess, look away, move on and move closer.

Make a note of any other animals present between you and your intended shooting destination that might get spooked along the way. For example, you might see a group of rabbits playing in a field about 80 yards away, but what if there is a crow in a tree halfway between you and the rabbits? If it is alarmed, it will flee the area and provide a signal to the rabbits that a predator is near. It might even be a good idea to shoot the crow first, if the shot seems a viable one. If shooting around the farmyard there can be all sorts of other animals – hens, chickens, geese, woodpigeon …, and all of them will signal your presence once they themselves become spooked.

Therefore, although it is important to identify your goal in terms of both quarry and intended destination, it is also vital that you maintain a broad awareness of your surroundings at all times, even if these other animals are not an intended target at this time.

If you are in an open field, stick to the perimeter hedgerow if there is one, and use it as a background to blend with for as long as possible to get close. Look for shadows projecting across the ground and stick to those, especially if you want to move more centrally into the field. A setting sun will cast shadows from trees and hedgerows into the field; use these to get close to things like rabbits. You might be surprised at how close to a rabbit you can get if it is in the sunny patch and you are in the shadows. Keep low and crouched down with the hedge behind you because this helps to ensure that you blend into the available background, as opposed to standing out against the background sky from the point of view of the rabbit (perspective-taking). It's not a competition for how close you can get – it's about stalking the animal into your effective range.

There might be occasions when you have to enter a certain space, like a field, through one specific point or gateway. It could be the only way in and sub-optimal in terms of getting into position for shooting your quarry, because the wind might be blowing your scent and noise toward them, and there is nothing you can do. You might begin stalking toward the rabbits and spook them, but don't worry. The trick here, once they have run off, is to turn the elements in your favour, place yourself in a more favourable position and simply wait. The rabbits will return after a given time period and start to feed again. The difference now is that you're ready and in place to optimise the elements in your favour. Sometimes, you just have to think of the bigger picture and spooking animals can be unavoidable whilst trying to implement your game plan. Even woodpigeons can return within a few tens of minutes. In this scenario, where it might be impossible to stalk, you've basically switched to an ambush strategy, which could be better suited to certain scenarios.

I remember once stalking a rabbit from 60 yards down to around 25 yards, both of us in the middle a field and me standing bolt upright in front of it, although with woodland behind me. It must have taken me 15–20mins in total to get this close. There were cows surrounding us, and as they broke the line of sight between the rabbit and me, I slowly walked toward it, stopping only when the cow had passed and then staying still and waiting for the next cow to come between us. It worked a treat, except – I must honestly confess – for completely pulling and missing the

HUNTING: FIELDCRAFT   6

shot at the end of it. Nonetheless, as a method for getting close, it worked really well and the rabbit was completely unaware I was there until my pellet whizzed an inch above its head and it ran off laughing. What a buzz this stalk was though! The idea of using the cows just came to me as I observed what was happening in the field, and I thought, 'why not try it'? In terms of getting close, it really worked.

Stalking is about stealth. It's about cutting down the distance between you and your intended target to ensure, as much as possible, that your shot is a successful and humane one. The landscape and the perceptual abilities of the wildlife itself will pose challenges, and these will need to be considered as and when they present themselves. You might find yourself stalking one animal, or a whole bunch of them, the latter being much harder because there are multiple pairs of eyes and ears on you. The animals also watch each other for cues and signs of being startled. If you watch a group of feeding rabbits, you will often see some with their heads down feeding, whilst others sit up and watch their surroundings. They work together to ensure that they do not become prey. Make sure you watch how they feed and what they are doing. If their heads are down munching, move forward toward them – they're alertness has lessened. The successful stalker will need to be aware of this and pay close attention to the behaviour of the animal.

For example, if a rabbit stops feeding and sits bolt upright looking straight at you, freeze and stay still. The rabbit has been alerted by something and is now hyper-vigilant. Wait – it is likely that it will return to its feeding and become relaxed again in good time, and this is the cue that you can resume the stalk. Similar principles apply to other animals. Pay close attention to their behaviour – are they relaxed and unaware, or skittish and alert? As you get closer you need to pay more attention to being quieter and moving more slowly. Think about the surroundings. Fast-flowing water from streams masks noise, as does wind. Use this to your advantage. If you spook a rabbit, typically the others will run as well, even though these other rabbits might not have even seen you.

Once within range, slowly shoulder the gun. Make sure the shot is safe, should you miss, and the gun is in its familiar position in your shoulder. Do not rush it or you will spook the animal. Use slow and continuous movements. Remain calm. Keep head movements to a minimum. Take careful aim and run through a few mental checks such as; making sure you're not cantering the gun, check you have a steady posture, the safety catch is now off and there actually is pellet loaded and ready to fire. Make sure there are no twigs or branches in the way of the shot or in front of the barrel. Consider the wind, angle, and distance and place the crosshairs in the right place, based on this assessment and the knowledge of your set-up. Gently pull the trigger and release the shot. The stalk is a successful one if the animal has been swiftly and humanely dispatched without it ever having been aware of your presence.

A grey squirrel appears scurrying down a tree trunk. For this, I kneeled and used the thicket bush in front of me for extra concealment. I poked the barrel through an opening so not to hamper the pellet on its trajectory to the squizzer some 20 yards away. The squirrel was cautious and paused halfway down the tree trunk, presenting me with a perfect head shot opportunity.

THE ART OF AMBUSHING

It is often said that patience is a virtue. It is also one of the hunters' main attributes. Pest species rarely throw themselves at you and present you with the gift of a great shot with little effort on your part. One of the central principles of successful hunting

HUNTING: FIELDCRAFT   6

with airguns is the concept of ambush. Assuming you have put your practice in and can achieve good groupings at respectable hunting distances, then your efficacy is certainly confirmed – at least on the practice range. The trick now is applying this skill in the field, and ambushing is one way when the proficient airgunner comes into their own. It is a devastating method when applied correctly.

Successful ambushing requires two main things; finding a location where the quarry of interest is often found, and working out an optimal ambush position from which to hit the unsuspecting quarry in that location – so successful ambushing requires prior research. Most species are creatures of habit and prefer to feed in places familiar and common to them, thus giving the hunter all the information they need in terms of where to encounter them next time. As noted elsewhere in this book, ambushing can encompass using hides, baiting and feeding, using camo-netting, decoying, or simply ensuring that you are well concealed whilst having an excellent view of the critical area.

For ambushing, do your research and pick your place – then wait. Good concealment will help to ensure success.

Irrespective of method, you need to know *where* to ambush. If it's woodpigeons you have decided to hit, then looking for sitty trees, likely covered in excrement and feathers snagged in branches or on the ground, and establishing flight paths is important. For rabbits, locating the burrows, signs of rabbit runs and droppings, will all signal areas of bunny activity and tell you clearly where the animals frequent. The trick now is to locate an ambush position. The farmyard will present many ambush opportunities. Here, the buildings, tractors, and machinery could all be used to provide cover for the ambusher, providing their configuration co-exists with viable kill spaces. These have the added advantage of being highly familiar to the quarry and so nothing should seem out of the ordinary to them.

LEFT: *Foraging on the orchard ground, totally oblivious to my presence some 30 yards away. For the perfect ambush, a good position should give both outstanding concealment and an excellent view of the prescribed kill space. Sitting on my shooting seat, concealed by camouflage clothing and hidden in the foliage, with a tuned airgun resting in a shooting stick, the odds are clearly stacked against the squirrel.*

LEFT: *The perfect ambush. In woodlands, fallen trees can provide the perfect natural hide and ambush site. Get close to them, stay low and keep movements to a minimum once in place. If the woodland provides such gems in quarry-rich regions, these can be added to with camo-leaf netting and hide work to take the effect further. The summer months would provide even more coverage, although the principle is the same.*

HUNTING: FIELDCRAFT

Ideally, the distance between chosen shooting location, and that of the quarry will be well within optimal airgun ranges. A closer distance might help with precision, but an increased distance will help with concealment – as always, it's an act of balancing these opposing attributes. There will always be exceptions, but the idea is to optimise distance into ideal airgun ranges. The real skill is getting close with an airgun – circa 25–30 yards – and that's why fieldcraft is so important. I'm more impressed by the hunter who successfully stalks the quarry down from 50 to 25 yards than the hunter who takes the shot on at 50 yards for no reason.

Being hidden is very important for all types of ambushing, but this is not always possible. Around the farm buildings there are lots of opportunities, but out in the open fields these are harder to come by. One effective way to ambush rabbits, if there is no other suitable cover, is to lie on your belly about 30 yards or so from the warrens, but directly facing them. You need to lie low and stay still not to be noticed – first ensure that the wind is not blowing from behind you and toward the warrens. The idea is to shoot from a fully prone position, either from a bipod or using your rucksack as a rest because this will give you the advantage of perhaps the most stable and accurate shooting position. The disadvantage is, you are lying on your belly in a cold, sometimes muddy field – not ideal – but if you're shooting a PCP, then a bipod fitted to the airgun makes this a deadly method. It is also a good idea to make sure that if you are going to be spending a long time lying on your belly, or sitting in hedgerows, you've protected yourself from bites. Always check yourself for bites and ticks after being on forays when you suspect there could be a risk.

HUNTING IN WOODLANDS

Hunting in woodland can certainly be challenging, always rewarding, and represents a collection of very specific skills, including stalking and ambushing. It is a many-varied environment and by far my favourite type of hunting terrain. One can go from dense collections of trees and foliage to wide open spaces in a few tens of yards. If you are new to shooting a particular region of woodland one of the first things to do is survey the area and get to know it.

Ask yourself, what type of foliage is available – evergreen and/or deciduous trees? What about natural pathways through the woodland? Assess the hazards, swampy areas to avoid, ravines, and so on. Crucially, look for signs of the presence of certain animals, such as dreys, bark stripping too high to be deer, and eaten acorns – all suggesting the presence of grey squirrels – ring barking low on tree trunks, scratching or scrapes on the ground sometimes with droppings, runs through the vegetation on the ground, fur clumps snagged on brambles or twigs, the presence of active burrows and warrens – all suggestive of rabbits. Possible 'sitty' trees (woodpigeon) which tend to be high, fairly bare, with lots of white excrement splashed down the tree or on the ground implying it is used a lot. Sitty trees can be in the middle of woodland, providing some seclusion as well as a good localised view, or on the perimeter, providing less seclusion but a good view of the feeding areas, but they will always be fairly tall and fairly bare. Are there any raptors nearby? These may signal the presence of small mammals on which they feed. Listen for sounds. Can you hear woodpigeons cooing or landing in trees, with that distinctive set of brief 'claps'? What about foxes barking? Not that we are interested in foxes, but if they are around, what they prey on might be as well – i.e., rabbits, and so on. Once you know what to look and listen for, these cues can be used by the hunter to improve and optimise their efficacy in that space.

Visit the woodland early in the morning and at dusk. Having delineated what might be the productive spaces in the woodland, it is now important to establish a series of approaches to these various spaces. You could now also help things by removing noisy foliage hampering your movement through certain routes, trimming branches, building hides, or putting up netting so that the environment is optimised. Trimming branches can also be useful for clearing a way for shots to travel unimpeded to the target. By doing this, your movement should be quieter in terms of what is on the ground. Twigs and branches can sound like walking on broken glass at times, and are sure to give away your position if stepped on. Brushing past branches can generate noise. This is another reason for using top-quality clothing which should be made of a very quiet material. It is important to consider clearing some common pathways of offending materials to allow for a more stealthy approach, but do not over-trim the area.

The ideal situation is one that gives good coverage so that you can get close to your intended region, but avoids noisy clambering through overly thick overgrowth. Visiting the woods after a storm can be productive because it provides the hunter with plenty of fallen branches that can be collected and placed or fashioned into hides. Over time, hunters learn how to make small adjustments to optimise various places on the land they shoot.

HUNTING: FIELDCRAFT

You can decide whether to move around the woodland slowly, to target a certain area and hold up for a while in regions you suspect might be productive, or do both at different times on the same foray. If you have been shooting the area for a while, chances are you've built some hides at various places, and as noted above, possibly even cleared away some sources of noise. It is also good practice to ensure that there are no branches interfering with a wide angle of possible shots from pre-chosen positions. If you have not done this yet, then you might want to consider it for future visits.

When stalking through the woods, keep movement slow but fluid and stop every few steps to survey the environment carefully – it is easier to spot movement in your environment if you are still. Woodlands are great for providing you with lots of cover, but they do the same for the animals you are interested in culling as well. You could be surrounded by many species and be completely unaware of it due to the dense and cluttered field of view. Take your time to scan the visual world and listen to the sounds around you. While you are still, look for movement. Keep head movements slow as you move through the woods. Scan the ground a few feet ahead of you for potential hazards you could step on, and then again a bit further ahead of you for animals on the move. Scan the tree canopy as well as you move slowly through the wood.

Dense conifers are common in woodland. Shooting into such trees is difficult due to the thick and year-round coverage they provide. The trick here is to wait or lure the animals out of the protection of the evergreen foliage and on to the ground, through decoying pest birds or setting up feeding stations near these trees for grey squirrels. Set up your ambush position in relation to your kill space on the ground, but make sure you also have excellent concealment relative to animals that might be watching you from the safety of their own position.

Light levels will be lower in dense forest. In addition, the last of the daylight will be felt earlier due to the trees cutting a good deal of light from illuminating the woodland area. For me, an illuminated scope reticle is an absolute must for hunting in woodland. The black, thin crosshairs are easy to lose sight of when you are looking through the scope scanning thick tree canopies, dense branches, or dark areas, and even more so in lower light. A mild degree of illumination can make things much easier when trying to place the crosshairs on the animal under such circumstances.

Taking shots in woodland also requires an assessment of the pellet path between gun and animal. Remember the trajectory of the pellet relative to your crosshairs

6 THE AIRGUNNER'S COMPANION

Top Left: *Stalking through woodland – a technique that will test your standing shooting because sometimes kneeling or sitting will not provide a clear path to the target. The standing stance is the hardest to master so be sure to put the practice in on this one.*

Left: *Even in patches of woodland with very little cover, sticking close to large objects like trees can be helpful, but remember to stay still as the bunnies emerge. Once you've located them, give them a little time to settle before shouldering the gun and taking the shot. You might get more than one if you allow them to split up and settle first. Be patient.*

Bottom Left: *A lack of natural cover, as in winter shooting, is not the end of the world. Use the geometric lines available in the environment and place or align yourself close to them. This will help you to blend with your surroundings. From the perspective of the animal – a rabbit or squirrel – you will be almost invisible providing you make no sudden movements. Other species, like woodpigeons and crows, will need much more convincing than this!*

HUNTING: FIELDCRAFT 6

and spare a thought to whether this might bring the pellet into contact with twigs or branches, and so deflecting the pellet significantly away from the intended target. Looking through the scope is not always sufficient because close twigs will be out of focus and almost invisible. Try to place your barrel in front of nearby obstacles, or trim/move them if possible.

Some of the woodland I shoot in is vast or remote. It is wise to take a few basic provisions with you so you do not need to keep running back and forth to the car, and you can stay out longer. It is also easy to lose track of time when you are out enjoying yourself and it is important not to get the munchies when you are a good distance from refreshments. I always take a chocolate bar should I need a hit of energy and glucose. I also have a sandwich, and a flask of coffee and if I'm feeling really plush – I enjoy a small, cold pork pie! In one pocket I will also take a small provision of toilet paper and its use should not require discussion here! Make sure you wear a watch and take a torch, even if you are hunting during the day. The light can leave you quickly, and if you lose track of time, you might still be caught up on a hillside somewhere in rapidly diminishing light. Remember to have your knife on you so that animals can be gutted quickly, and for any light fieldwork that might be needed. Equipped in this way, I can stay out for most of the day or evening with no problem.

Shooting in woodlands is a very enriching, rewarding, and satisfying experience. You can be surrounded by a symphony of sounds, a wealth of different and pleasing smells – wet grass, leaves, soil – and a legion of visual treats. It can be an assault on the senses, but a good one.

Try to establish more than one route to take through the woods, and use them all so that any spooked animals do not get overly used to a pattern associated with your presence. Ideally, have multiple routes to the same productive places. Flowing water from white-water streams can mask any noise you generate, allowing you to get closer to certain animals – woodpigeons or rabbits – providing you are still concealed visually. The wind rattling through the high tree canopy can have a similar effect, although the very same wind could impact on the accuracy of your shot. If you are shooting up into the tree canopy, be aware of the shooting angle and the necessary compensations – shoot lower – you might need to apply to your shots. It is often a good idea that once in position, you take a few practice shots to note the degree of compensation required for a certain elevation at a certain distance.

SHOOTING AROUND THE FARMYARD

There is some great shooting to be had around the farmyard. There are also specific factors to be aware of when shooting in this context. Always be conscious of who and what is about on the farm while you are there. It could be that certain animals have been brought out of the fields into various enclosures; new-borns are in pens, and even farm workers might be walking around. Ideally, you'll be shooting at times when farm workers are not around, or at least not as much, but remember it's a working farm and things change all the time. You need to be hyper-vigilant for potential hazards. Never take a shot without considering what will happen if you miss. Ask yourself, is the pellet safe or will it travel into an unsafe area? What are the chances of a ricochet? Will it go straight through a window or glass pane? What livestock are nearby? Make sure you answer these questions in your mind before committing to pulling the trigger.

Farmyards can be cluttered with all sorts of materials and machinery, so make sure you do not damage any of it. Always let the farmer know when you are on-site and wandering around the buildings. Either park the car in a certain place so he/she knows you're about, or contact them the day before to let them know. This is also particularly the case when shooting at night around the buildings. The farmer needs to know the lamp he can see flashing about is the hunter he has allowed on his land, and not a burglar or sheep rustler!

Shooting around the farmyard does not require camouflage. Leaving aside what has been discussed elsewhere in this book concerning camouflage, most farmyards consist of concrete buildings, corrugated iron sheeting, metal structures, machinery, vehicles, plastic, some foliage, and a host of other objects and materials. Camouflage is unlikely to help break up the human shape against this backdrop, but it is still important to wear subdued colours – blacks, dark blues, greens, browns – whilst wandering around as this will still provide sufficient concealment. You can also give your cheap wellington boots or stalking boots a try around what is often a muddy or waterlogged area – trainers will struggle to cope unless the ground is bone dry.

Some species that frequent the farmyard and outbuildings are very used to seeing humans about the place and will often perceive no threat. This is probably based on the fact that most farm workers are busy doing their jobs and not talking shots at the collared doves, woodpigeons, rooks, jackdaws, or crows. This means you can get close without needing to be nearly invisible, but don't take liberties. The quarry

HUNTING: FIELDCRAFT   6

Spaces like this old barn provide lots of sanctuary for a variety of pest bird species including rooks, jackdaws, feral and woodpigeon. Such quarry will prefer the high beams and high recesses in the stone walls. Think carefully about your shots before taking them. Ask yourself, where will my pellet go if I miss? Do I have a safe backstop? What are the chances of a ricochet? In addition, remember to compensate in your aiming points to accommodate the likely effects of reduced gravity on your pellet's trajectory due to such steep angles.

are aware of you, but you might get away with a little more around the farmyard. Prior research really helps with shooting around farm buildings because you can work out a few different routes leading toward productive areas, and a few good ambush points in which to sit and wait. It's also a good idea to use the laser rangefinder on a few landmarks around the place, so you know the distance to markers, from certain shooting positions. This will take the guesswork out of distance judgements and make you more agile whilst you are shooting 'on the fly', so to speak, around the farmyard.

Shooting around farm buildings can be really rewarding and does indeed require fieldcraft skills. You can wander around and see unsuspecting quarry taking a nap, or sunning themselves from feeding out in the fields. You might get lucky with their reduced alertness, but you still need to be able to stalk to get them within range, in many cases. Alternatively, you can set yourself up in a farm building or barn and wait for the incoming woodies or collared doves that are looking for free food. Impromptu hides, shooting seats, and supports can be provided by machinery, tractors, trailers, and farm products left lying around the place. Make yourself comfortable, sit and wait in an area giving you an excellent and safe shooting angle into a productive kill space. I've shot countless collared doves and woodpigeon that come out around the buildings, or perch on or near drinking troughs at certain times of the day. It can be highly enjoyable and productive – providing you with new challenges around every corner.

LAMPING

Lamping is particularly effective on rabbits. Rats can be lamped as well, but lamping is a method at its most devastating with rabbits. There are lots of lamping systems out there you can use and they are all very good at what they do. An integrated, scope-mounted system is very useful, compact and my current preferred type of system. Most are well made, light, rugged, waterproof, and do the job well, so the actual unit you pick is really just down to personal choice. There is no 'best unit', but modern systems should not include large batteries and lots of wires. If they are scope-mounted they should not affect the balance of the gun, as they once did years ago.

There is a skill to lamping effectively, but such methods are nothing more than a guide that will work most, but not all of the time. There are no hard and fast 'rules', just general guidelines to try. There are many things that can impact on the success of a lamping foray, including how well lamped the quarry are, whether the animals have been disturbed earlier that night, the weather, a full moon, wind or no wind, the time of the year, and your technique in the field.

The first step in effective lamping has nothing to do with the lamping itself, but is concerned with an assessment of the 'to be lamped' area during the daylight hours. Prior research here includes things like locating the warrens, the runways the rabbits typically take – narrow paths of flattened grass – and scratchings on the ground, bare pockets of earth often filled with excrement. Locate and identify these signs and you will soon get a feel for the field at night, and where the rabbits are likely to be. In the darkness, rabbits use smell and other senses – familiar rabbit runs – to navigate their way to and from the warrens, so look for signs of droppings and well-used pathways.

When it comes to the lamping later on, the real trick is to have the lamp on for as little time as possible. The first step is to scan the area, for eyes reflecting back at you. Make sure what you are looking at is a rabbit and not a cat, fox or badger. For scanning the fields, the lamp needs to be bright and used with care. Do not flash the beam all over the place, or you will spook most of the rabbits. When spotting them from distance you do not even need the centre mass of the beam on them. I like to drop the light down onto an area, rather than shake it about side-to-side, which can generate moving shadows and again, might spook the rabbits.

Many hunters swear by the use of red or amber filters, and it is true that rabbits cannot see those colours, but they will still be aware of the brightness of the lamp, so this is not a foolproof system. I've never really been overly aware of any real advantage, although I have certainly had success with both a white lamp and one attached with filters. My current and 'on balance' view is that even if filters do help, it would be wrong to think that rabbits are unaware of the lamp when switched on. They will still perceive the brightness of the light being switched on to some degree and might react to it. Luminance and hue are not the same thing. Simply using a dimmer light setting can work as well as filters when taking the shot, and most modern units should have a luminance adjustment on them. I've enjoyed a lot of success when taking the shot under an intermediate or low level of brightness.

Bunnies will do one of four things when being lamped; they will run off and scarper; sit still and freeze – sit low, tuck their ears down, and hope for the best; become confused and run towards the lamp; or show no awareness of the lamp whatsoever and carry on doing what they were doing. The latter three scenarios are more typical of early season rabbits and this behaviour is most fatal. When lamping fields riddled with rabbits, don't chase the runners; stick to those sitting fast, doing nothing, or running toward you all confused. The skill is in knowing which rabbits to stay focused on in a field literally crawling with them. Very still nights, and those when there is a full or bright moon, can spoil a night's lamping in some cases because rabbits will both hear and see you far too soon. By all means give it a try, but don't be disappointed when the bag you return with is not as full as you'd hoped. In general, the darker the night, the better for lamping, and you really need a bit of wind blowing in the right direction, into your face or a crosswind between you and the warrens. On the whole, the presence of some wind is helpful, but remember to use this to your advantage.

If you're scanning fields and spot red eyes at distance, kill the light and stalk toward their position. Be careful and be quiet – they are still likely to be there. However, the loss of light does not reduce their sense of smell, their sense of vibration through the ground, or hearing. If anything, it is you at the disadvantage in darkness. Once you are much closer, turn the lamp back on, maybe you're in range, maybe not. If the rabbit is in range and it makes some initial movement indicating that it's about to run, wobble the light around just a little to confuse it, whilst keeping it on the rabbit to some degree. It might freeze again, stay still, be in range, and then you're set to take the shot.

On occasion, you can shine the lamp into the area the rabbit is slowly hopping toward, and often they will turn away from the illuminated area on the ground, change direction, and might well come closer to you, so it is possible to shepherd them in this way from time to time. If there is only one shot on, it's worth tracking the rabbit if it is running, or just hopping along toward the warrens. Eight times out of ten the rabbit will pause before finally jumping through the fence or hedge out of sight, and that's often all the time you need.

Another neat trick is to kiss the back of your hand loudly, whistle, or do a loud 'kiss' noise with your lips as it is running. This can often mimic the sound of a rabbit in distress and the runner might pause, sit up, and be well within range, staying still long enough for you to squeeze that shot off. Never think your opportunity is lost until you have full visual evidence. The shot is always on, until Roger disappears.

Finally, while all your attention has been on the rabbit that ran away, do not despair. There might still be one, and possibly a more preferable shot to the one you fixated on. It could simply be better hidden, but still frozen in the field, so always recheck the area for eyes on the ground before giving up and moving on. If rabbits are just out of range, but frozen down tight in the grass, keep the light on them and stalk them a few yards into range. On the whole they will not move if confused by the lamp, unless you get too close and they smell or hear you. A few lamping sessions will give you a real feel for what I'm describing here, and you will develop some techniques and methods of your own. In the modern world, many have moved on to night-vision for night-time shooting, but don't believe anyone telling you lamping is not effective for rabbits. They have been effectively lamped for decades, and it's a very effective method. Night-vision might have its own attributes and advantages, but lamping works, and can be a much cheaper and more practical alternative for many.

HUNTING: FIELDCRAFT

FEEDING AND BAITING

Baiting works with many pests, but two pest species that respond well to feeding or baiting methods are rats and grey squirrels. Rats are typically nocturnal or dusk feeders, although they can be around throughout the day if undisturbed. The old favourite for targeting rats is to use liquidised cat food. Get it as watery as possible and add anything to it that is as stinky as possible – fish oil from tinned salmon or tuna, for example. The more repulsive the mix, the better the result. The consistency of water is the final desired state, no chunks. On the first night, put some of this food down on the concrete floor in a pre-chosen place. Do this for a few nights in a row, allowing the rats to learn that a free meal is available in that specific place and that it is safe for them to eat it. On the final night, do the same, only now be ready in your also pre-chosen ambush position – about 15 yards away for rats – giving you the best seat in the house. Ratty will come for his supper as he has done the last few times, only now he is in for a surprise.

    This is a great method in itself, and very effective if coupled to night-vision. If your intention is to lamp the rats, then leaving a barn light on for the first few nights will at least get them used to seeing a light and not running off immediately when you switch yours on. The watery nature of the feed means that the rat has to pause to lap up the food. That's just long enough for you to squeeze a shot off. If there are chunks in the food the rat will be super-fast at running to the food, picking up the chunk, and running off to eat it, so you'll need to be Spaghetti-Western quick to nail them. It's preferable to slow them down as much as you can in the first place.

    Grey squirrels also respond well to placing feeding stations in woodland, and feeders can work all year round. Studies have shown that squirrels alter their feeding behaviour based on their assessment of coverage and the potential presence of predators, so in some cases, squirrels will take food and run off and eat it under cover, perhaps not giving the hunter much time for a considered shot. In other cases, they might just sit there giving you all the time in the world, so the placement of feeders is something that requires careful thought. The squirrel might not take to it if it feels vulnerable, or under threat from predators like raptors. Place a feeder in an area that provides a lot of nearby coverage for the squirrel should it feel the need for it.

    It is important to consider the shooting position when placing feeders. You need good concealment, but also a safe back-stop and you do not want to be facing the feeder head-on to your shooting position. Most squirrel feeders have ledges on the front of them, and it is best to have these orientated three-quarters-on, to side-on, so that if you miss you don't shoot your own feeder!

Other species might have established their own feeding stations, such as feeding from crops in certain fields or grain stored on the farm. Once these spots have been identified, it's a case of establishing ambush positions, using cover to target them. For animals like woodpigeons, pay particular attention for 'sitty trees' – trees that groups of birds use repeatedly to sit in, rest and watch over things. If you're in position for their next visit to the tree, you could be in for a good day's shooting. Sitty trees tend to be tall and fairly bald of leaves and foliage so that the birds can see their surroundings. To be effective at hitting sitty trees you will need a good degree of concealment, and if the natural coverage is not excellent – and I mean excellent – use camo-netting or a hide of some sort. For me, effective woodpigeon and crow shooting is the sign of an efficient and knowledgeable hunter. Success with these animals does not come easy.

Crows and magpies can also be targeted effectively with a dead rabbit or grey squirrel carcass. To do this, gut the rabbit and leave its innards hanging out. Place the rabbit on its back with the white of its belly showing upwards and all its internals on show. You might want to add a decoy or two as well. Now go hide in your pre-prepared location and wait patiently.

AN OPTIMISED FEEDER-BASED APPROACH FOR GREY SQUIRRELS

Hoping to get lucky by randomly walking through the woods looking for grey squirrels is not an optimal strategy for making serious inroads into culling their numbers. You might get a couple, but as a method it is far from effective. One very proficient method is to use a feeder-based approach, often called a bait-station, and there are ways to optimise this method further, thus maximising its efficacy. Here is a discussion of some of the important things to consider and how to optimise a feeder-based approach for effective grey squirrel hunting as part of serious conservation projects.

HUNTING: FIELDCRAFT   6

THE USE OF ZONES:

If the woodland is large and substantial, it is a good idea to use a map to define different zones to target, or do this in your mind as a mental exercise. Once done, explore those zones and seek to locate the dreys in that area, if possible. Nest-type dreys are not hard to find in the winter months, but grey squirrels also use hollow trees and branch holes as nesting sites, and these are not always easy to locate. Nonetheless, it is useful to engage in a bit of drey spotting if it can be done. Now, you could put feeders into all zones simultaneously – near to the dreys if they are known – and monitor which feeders are enjoying the most activity, but keeping all the feeders topped up can be costly, both financially and in terms of time, and if the feeders are too close together, the chances are that it's the same squirrels hitting all the feeders.

Alternatively, simply set up one feeder, and if it receives no activity over a 10-day period, consider relocating it, or maybe, if it's been inadvertently set in the wrong place within the zone, seek to pick a better one in the local proximity. Irrespective of how you chose to address it, in large woodland it is helpful to establish zones when trying to delineate where the grey squirrels are most densely populated, and to get a feel of the areas you will need to move into over the coming months. Large projects require a strategic approach.

As activity in your chosen location drops or stops completely, using zones helps to inform your next choices, allowing you to keep track of where you've been. This makes your approach more systematic and easier to assess in terms of working out the presence and number of grey squirrels in the woodland. These issues are less important with more humble-sized woodland where perhaps only one feeder, well placed, is all that is ever required. In this situation, the use of zones is redundant.

FEEDER TYPE

Designs vary greatly for squirrel feeders. Personally, I don't like those where the feed itself is in the open, in some kind of tray, because birds and other species can help themselves to your feed. I prefer the wooden flip-top lid variety with a clear Perspex front window where the feed is secured inside a reservoir. Birds will still come to it because squirrels are messy eaters and will spread nuts and seeds over the feeder and floor, but that's OK – the unintended species are not taking all the food, just the left-overs.

Once a squirrel has learned to use them you can hear the sound of the lids flopping through the woods and you know that the feeders are being hit, which is useful if your attention is elsewhere at the time. It is also easy to see the level of feed and whether or not it needs topping up, from a distance. If made of wood, these feeders will degrade naturally over time, or take some hammer (chewing) from the squirrels themselves. This can be offset by the use of metal trimmings or wire mesh attached, but even without them I can get wooden feeders to last around two or three years before they need swapping out – which is fine and tolerable. Many red squirrel conservation groups make feeders for their volunteer rangers and these tend to be better made than commercially available ones, so it is worth considering joining such groups and helping out with these initiatives.

How Many Feeders?

This is a tricky question to answer. Obviously, the size of the woodland to be covered is important, as well as the presence of nearby woodland. One source of information to help inform our decisions is to take the foraging range of an individual squirrel, and map this to the size of the woodland we are covering, or the size of the woodland and the distance or range of immediate neighbouring woods. Grey squirrels will forage over a much wider region than that of the red squirrel, and for both species, males cover a larger region than females. Estimates vary on the scope of foraging behaviour and this is influenced by a host of factors including; the season, the density of squirrels in the area, the presence of predators, the habitat, including tree species and their spatial distribution, which also dictates the quality of localised food sources, and the provision of safe refuge. Put simply, if the food sources are poor and the density of squirrels low, then the total home ranges of the squirrels in that area are larger and will extend much further. This means you could get visits on your feeder from squirrels travelling from quite far away, as well as more local ones. If the food sources are abundant and of excellent quality, if there are lots of sources of refuge, and there are few threats, then the squirrels in the area will have much lower total foraging ranges. Why go looking for food if it's in abundance on your doorstep?

Having acknowledged these sources of influence, let us consider some generalised observations. The total range of a grey squirrel can be categorised into two components;

a 'core' range, where most of its activity occurs, and an 'outer' or total range, where it will extend to when foraging if needs be. Early research suggested that the total home range, or 'outer' range, of an individual grey squirrel was around 0.49–0.72 hectares, with the greatest lateral distance between drey and core range being around 140 metres. However, more recent research, using radio tracking methods, suggests that the total home range of the grey squirrel could be between 5 to 8 hectares (ha) with a core range of less than 2ha. Interestingly, the core range estimates are the same for both red and grey squirrels, although the total range is much larger for the grey squirrel.

These general figures, mediated by the sources of variability discussed above, can all influence what might be the optimal number of feeders to place in a given wood or a particular area. My general advice would be to assess the scope and size of the woodland, investigate the signs of activity, and start small with a single feeder, placed under consideration, and build from that solid foundation. Should you feel more feeders are required due to the scope of the project, the size of woodland or how ferociously the feeder is being hit, then these can be added to as the project grows. As a general rule of thumb, I'd recommend one feeder per 2ha of constant woodland. There is no need to put multiple feeders in short range of each other because all this will do is make the same squirrels fractionate their activity across multiple feeders, and all we really want to achieve here is a feeding spot for all the squirrels in that area. Of course, that is unless the squirrels are so high in number that they are chasing each other too much when they come into feed, due to a bottleneck in the provision of peanuts!

Food Mix

For the feeders, a basic and effective squirrel mix can include peanuts and maize, with some seeds for scent: e.g., sunflower hearts or pine nuts. Interestingly, red squirrels do not generally eat maize, so if you're shooting in regions where red squirrels might be present, maize being eaten suggests the presence of greys. Maize mixed with nuts can work well. Grey squirrels will often ignore the maize during summer and simply throw it on the floor, although sometimes they still nibble on the kernel of it. I tend to find pure maize does not work well on its own, so while its financially good to use, add more nuts and goodies. A good bias would be 80% nuts and sweet things, 20% maize.

Any mix can be complemented further by a scent attractant, which helps to establish a new feeder in that area, drawing the squirrels in to feed. I use Nutella which seems to work very well, although I'm sure any nut-based spread would suffice. I smear this on the tree bark and on the inside of the flip-top lid in an effort to get the squirrels to learn how the feeder works as they try to get at it. I also throw some of the mix into the Nutella spread on the tree bark so that it 'sticks', providing extra goodies in the area and boosting the scent. This is also good to do at the start of a shooting session. When the greys come in to feed, they will go to the tree bark for the nutty goodies and present the hunter with a perfect, vertical headshot, impacting in through the top of their skull – the weakest part – so such approaches are designed to provide optimal solutions even in terms of trying to get the grey squirrel into a perfect position.

A good tip at the start of a session on the feeder, is to add monkey nuts to the mix occasionally, because the squirrel will often pause to nibble open the outer casing to get at the inner peanut. They tend to stay reasonably still when doing this, providing an ideal opportunity for an unhurried head shot, killing the quarry cleanly and humanely. You only need to add the monkey nuts when you arrive for a session of shooting because its sole purpose is to help provide a stationary shot. On occasion, the squirrel might run off with the monkey nut, but don't worry, it will return and won't do that all the time, preferring instead to have a nibble every once in a while. That's your opportunity.

One important point to note is if the squirrel behaviour on or around the feeder is particularly jittery and the squirrel is unsettled – grabbing food, running off very fast and not caching. If this occurs it suggests that the feeder is not placed in the best position – for some reason, the squirrel might not feel safe. If this happens, and you are concerned that the greys are not settling, consider changing the location of the feeder. It might only require moving the feeder on the same tree, maybe rotating it around the trunk, or putting it on another nearby tree, so the necessary change might only be marginal – not huge. Conversely, you might need to move on to a new area completely to enjoy better results. Observation of their behaviour should tell you when you've got it right. If they feel safe and comfortable, they should sit and take time to nibble, enjoying the free meal.

I have witnessed raptors swoop in on feeding squirrels, which makes them scarper sharpish, and if this situation persists, one can hardly blame the squirrel for not feeling safe on your feeder.

HUNTING: FIELDCRAFT

ABOVE LEFT AND MIDDLE: *If you get everything right, then whole groups of squirrels will descend on the feeder and engage in all sorts of frivolity.* ABOVE RIGHT: *They soon learn how to work the feeder so that they can get at the nutty goodies inside.*

Your squirrel feed will likely change through the year, and it should. In the late summer and early autumn months, squirrels will have access to lots of food in the woodland, so you'll need to add goodies to attract them in and compete with the banquet on offer more broadly. During this period, the woodland goes through a period known as 'masting' when the trees produce their fruit and nuts. The annual climate can impact on the quality of masting which can, in turn, impact on visits to your feeders. At the very least, increase the ratio of peanuts and add sweet things like some dried fruit. Peanuts will always work, but there can be periods when they are not top of the menu. More robust offerings also work well like shelled nuts – hazelnuts, chestnuts, walnuts, acorns – added to your standard mix in autumn time because this also encourages caching behaviour. In fact, believe it or not, but grey squirrels actually engage more in caching behaviour than eating during the late autumn period. Adding shelled nuts to your food mix gives the squirrel more than one reason to visit the feeder, and provides opportunities for shooting when they are on the ground trying to bury food.

The grey squirrel is a 'scatter hoarder' and will bury robust-shelled nuts individually in separate singular stashes in the ground – which they retrieve in the winter months based on spatial memory and to a lesser extent, smell. Squirrels are known to base their decision on whether to cache or not based on two main criteria; how perishable the food is, and its handling time – how long it's in the hands in order to be gnawed at and eaten. They can also assess whether food will survive being cached or not.

Peanuts will not survive and they know this, so as they become drawn toward caching behaviour, they tend to seek out food that will survive. This is why adding some robust-shelled nuts to your mix is a good thing at this time. Squirrels might not visit your feeder as much if it's just got perishable peanuts in there because it can get the more robust stuff from the woodland, and during late autumn the squirrel's brain is telling it to start caching and to feed less. This is why it is a good idea to have a proper 'mix' in the feeder, providing the squirrel with options at this time of the year. So, I'd suggest experimenting with your food mix through the year, as well as keeping them intellectually stimulated as they sift through the mix. Keep the peanuts and seeds in there for instant food because they certainly do want to feed during this time, but as stated above, at certain times add a wider variety of shelled and more robust nuts. The squirrel can then come to the feeder whether it wants to feed or stash. Either way, it's a big mistake!

ABOVE LEFT AND MIDDLE: *One of my squirrel mixes (peanuts, sunflower hearts, black sunflower hearts, monkey nuts, pine nuts) and my own squirrel feeder at the bottom of a garden. Note, the squirrel holds its position while it nibbles through the outer shell of a monkey nut. This provides the hunter with the perfect side-on, head shot opportunity.*

ABOVE RIGHT: *My autumn squirrel mix (containing peanuts, walnut kernels, pine nuts, hazelnuts, various seeds, monkey nuts, dried fruit etc, I also manually add whole walnuts to the feeder – not shown). Some items are there for instant food, some are for smell and some for caching. To make life easy I prepare portions in large freezer bags and take these out to the woods to top up the feeders.*

You can encourage caching behaviour by adding these more robust food sources by mid-September to your mix, or a bit earlier or later depending on noticeable changes in the weather. Be aware that when engaged in this behaviour, grey squirrels will be on the feeder for a very short period of time – they will pick the nut, assess it quickly and run off, so you'll need to be super-quick! Don't worry if the squirrel is gone in a flash, he'll be back and will engage in this behaviour for some considerable time so you'll get plenty of opportunities. The squirrel will also actually stop to feed from time to time, of course, so be ready for that because it will pause whilst feeding.

In the winter, they will be on the ground a lot, looking for the food they have cached previously. This is still a good time to hit them because once they find their stash, they will sit still for long enough for a shot. It's not that they have lost interest in the feeder, just that they are hard-wired to locate the food they have cached a few months earlier, but they will get distracted by your feeder to some degree as well, so a feeder-based approach can still be a very effective method in the depths of winter.

One final point: It is important to keep the feeder clean. If the food mix contains perishable items like peanuts, wheat and seeds, they can go mouldy if not eaten. Squirrels will not visit a feeder when the food in it has perished to such an advanced state, so it's a good idea every now and then to empty the feeder completely, if the squirrels are not doing it for you, clean with boiling water, and replenish with new food. I take my coffee flask full of boiling water into the woods to do this if it is needed. It's not a problem if the food is being taken and the feeder is being hit aggressively, but it can become a problem if food is left. Replace uneaten food if it looks as if it's seen better days. Another way to try to prevent the need for this is to half fill feeders whilst trying to ascertain the numbers of squirrels in the area. This makes it less likely that food will be left. If you find the feeder is being emptied quickly, then fill with more feed on your visits to it.

FEEDER PLACEMENT

Some thought needs to be given to the placement of the feeder. There may well be lots of options in the woods in terms of placement, but there are some guiding principles to help ensure success. In an ideal world, it would be helpful to establish the location of dreys in the area, and place feeders near these – not the same tree as the drey, but close by. This is not always possible, but it can be worthwhile trying to ascertain the location of dreys as a first step. Grey squirrels also have established 'highways' through the woodland, be it in the tree canopy or the woodland floor. These are well-learned and trusted routes from drey to drey, or drey to feeding areas. Observing these highways and placing feeders along them will help to ensure that the feeder receives the attention you're trying to encourage.

One thing often overlooked, or not mentioned in squirrel hunting, but well known in animal biology, is that grey squirrels not only have specific highways through the woodland, but they also engage in what is called 'timetabling' behaviour. Timetabling basically refers to their use of their home range regions, but the different sections are visited at certain times, and they do this consistently, so basically, each region in a range is not only visited, but also visited in a specific order, like a bus route. This is why the use of trail cams can be helpful. Not only might you be revealing when the squirrel visits a feeder, but also, if you have a few cameras in the area, then the squirrels might have an order in which they engage with the different regions, and knowing that can really help with deciding where to be, and when.

Things get even more interesting; in large woodland, grey squirrels can completely shift their home ranges between the seasons, and there can be little if any overlap between seasonal ranges. This means that once you've established some of the highways through the trees, and placed feeders accordingly, this situation might not exist throughout the year. The hunter would be mistaken to think they have culled most numbers, or that other predators have intervened, if the number of sightings and visitations to the feeder suddenly drop off. It could be that the squirrels have simply moved on to more productive parts of the woodland for that time period in the year. This might not be much of an issue for medium and smaller woodlands, but if you suddenly see a big drop in visitations to your feeders, and you know you have not culled them all, then seasonal changes in home ranges could explain, at least in part, what you are experiencing. The presence of your feeder could prevent squirrels from moving on to other home ranges, to some degree, although you might still become aware of fewer visits to the feeder. Don't panic, stick at it because there will always be some visits, and the others will return in due course.

One good option is to select potential trees that exist in some form of small clearing in the wood. This clearing does not need to be huge because squirrels will feel vulnerable in wide open spaces, but needs to represent a bit more space relative to the immediate surrounding woodland. This gives you the advantage of being able to see more of the area in which the squirrel might pop into view, but also provides more shooting options as the squirrel comes into feed – less obstruction from surrounding

HUNTING: FIELDCRAFT

trees. If the feeder is placed in an area that is overly dense with trees, then broader shooting options are more limited.

I tend to like old, and often broad, deciduous trees that give multiple squirrels room to climb and play, to act as good hosts for the feeder, although obviously, this is not always possible. I also think about which side of the tree to place the feeder, so that the squirrel feels safe, and think about a safe backstop. Once a potential tree has been identified, it's important to consider the position of the shooter – from where are you going to ambush? Using what is naturally available is always a good idea, such as shaded areas or overhanging low branches rich in foliage and providing a natural canopy for you to sit underneath. In terms of distance, I'd suggest about 25 yards is optimal, no closer than about 19–20 yards if the cover is excellent, and no further away than 30 yards if at all possible.

It is also important to be aware of your surroundings and how these change over time. For example, on one squirrel feeder I set up my ambush position about 19 yards away from the feeder. This was closer than I would have liked, ideally, but the terrain in this case did not give me many options. Anyway, these decisions were made in May/June and the woodland grass was at waist height, giving lots of natural cover when I sat down on my bucket seat. This gave great squirrel shooting, and for around two months the greys never showed any awareness of my presence. Then the grass started to fall over and die off, and by August time, much of the cover I had come to rely on had gone, leaving me more exposed. I noticed that a few squirrels did indeed approach the feeder a little more gingerly, and I picked a few off as they were stationary and watching me from surrounding trees. The addition of some camo-leaf netting restored order on this one. The lesson here is to maintain awareness that the woodland is constantly changing through the year, and decisions made at certain times might require revision at others. Finally, remember to place the feeder at about chest level on the tree trunk to ensure that ground animals cannot raid or damage it.

Trail-Cameras

To optimise the method further, the feeder can be coupled with a passive infrared (PIR)-enabled trail camera to capture all visits. The use of trail cams is something of a game changer for feeder-based approaches because grey squirrels are creatures of habit, and it is now straightforward to establish their presence and feeding times whilst minimising the demands upon the time of the airgunner. Trail cams will reveal which squirrel species are present and when they like to feed. I've noticed some differences in behaviour across different woodlands so it is important to establish how the local squirrels are behaving, what times they really like to eat, and get an idea of how many are around. Once the data from the trail cams have been consulted and grey squirrel activity noted at a given feeder, then its ambush time!

ABOVE LEFT: *A fully prepared feeder located on an established 'highway' through the woodlands. It is filled with summer mix. Note also the peanuts wedged under the lid – to help the squirrel learn that the lid lifts – and the smearing of scent attractant in the tree bark itself with some of the mix impregnated into it. This can also attract birds, but that's a good thing because the squirrels are intrigued and relaxed by this, and the birds cannot get at the main reservoir of food.*

LEFT: *A trail camera set up toward a feeder a few yards away. All visits to the tree and feeder will be captured and stored with useful data to inform your next hunting foray.*

HUNTING: FIELDCRAFT   6

THE AMBUSH TECHNIQUE:

Grey squirrels are not nocturnal, preferring instead to feed in the early morning or early evening – known as 'diurnal behaviour'. Armed with the data from the trail cams – location, time of feeding, dates and so on – the planned ambush is now fully informed. The trick is to get out into the woods about 30 minutes before the squirrels

The discipline of employing a feeder-based strategy requires the airgunner to return regularly to the woodland, to keep them topped up so that the squirrels keep coming to them. If the feeders are left empty for too long then they need to be re-established in the area and you end up having to start all over again. You can use feeders with larger reservoirs of food, but remember, food can go mouldy in the woods due to the elements, so make sure it's well sealed. In addition, it's always good to have a reason to keep visiting the woods and keep an eye on things more generally.

come to feed, set up at your pre-chosen ambush point and simply wait. Be there before they are, otherwise they will see or hear you coming and scarper. Shooting seats and shooting sticks are very helpful here because it's important to be comfortable whilst waiting for the grey squirrels to come and feed. Extreme camouflage is not necessary for squirrels, although good concealment will always help, but cover the skin of your hands and face because these will stick out like a sore thumb in the woods, even more so in the winter woodland when there is less cover. Set up your shooting stick, take a practice shot at a leaf, an acorn, or something similar to ensure that you are zeroed, or to reveal any compensation in your pellets' trajectory you might require for the distance you've settled on, or the wind on the day. Use a laser rangefinder on a few landmarks around the place, to act as range markers for you when considering other shots that might present themselves. Now sit and wait patiently. All this research and preparation should pay significant dividends. Buckle in for some great shooting.

If you are shooting grey squirrels on feeders, in woodland where there are also red squirrels present, then it becomes important to disinfect the feeders regularly to prevent red squirrels becoming infected with the squirrel pox, which can be transmitted between the species. Trail cams will help pick up any activity indicating the presence of red squirrels. It is a very special experience to spot the red squirrel returning to woodland, but it does bring extra responsibilities with it in terms of using feeders.

DECOYING

One technique for effectively hunting both corvids and woodpigeons is decoying. Decoying works well on a number of bird species. Crows, magpies and woodpigeons all respond well when the technique is correctly implemented – it is a true art and one that deserves a volume on its own.

As with many hunting techniques, decoying requires prior research and observation. Do your research and establish favoured feeding places and the feeding times. Also, observe the pattern (spatial layout) of birds when they are feeding because you'll need to recreate this later with your decoys. In addition, it would be good if you could establish the location of nearby sitty trees because these can bear feathered fruit, if you catch my meaning. As well as established feeding spots, woodpigeons also have established flight paths in the sky that they like to use regularly. The late

HUNTING: FIELDCRAFT

John Darling once said that you should think of a field as if it's a room, with some doors for entering it and some doors for leaving it. Woodpigeons are not randomly flying into or out of the field; they are following established routes, and the hunter needs to understand these. So, it is worth spending some time researching these routes before picking where to build your hide and where to lay out your decoy pattern. In an ideal world, try to ensure that you set up your hide and decoys under an entering flight path. Putting a pattern of decoys out near to sitty trees can also be very effective – you can shoot just as many, if not more, in the sitty tree than on the ground. Unlike those using shotguns, the goal for the airgunner is to get the pigeon to land and be still, whether that's in the tree or on the ground.

There is no perfect number of decoys to use, but you need enough to establish a visual cue and pattern whilst not over-crowding the space. It often depends on how many live ones are around, and the pattern you are trying to establish on the ground, which should mimic the pattern you watched during your observation session. The whole fieldcraft of decoying is about identifying your kill area on the ground and using the decoys to funnel the live birds into that specific area – simple in principle! This kill area needs to be no further away than approximately 30 yards from the hide and the airgunner. This is a trade-off between keeping the distance far enough to help keep the hunter concealed, and keeping the distance close enough that the kill zone is an optimal distance for the airgun. Remember, the airgunner not only needs the birds to fly over the pattern, but to feel safe enough to land in the pattern and feed. In recent years, I've become a fan of flocked decoys, ones where the plastic decoy is covered in a kind of simulated texture. These appear more realistic and absorb or reflect the daylight more authentically.

For woodpigeons, another common view is to arrange the decoys into a general horseshoe pattern. To be honest, I tend to keep patterns fairly random while following the general guidance above about leaving spaces for the birds to fly into. Simply copying the pattern you observed naturally might be the best place to start, rather than trying to impose a forced pattern. The important principle is that if you lay things out one way, and it appears not to be working, there will come a time when you need to consider changing things and experimenting – hunters need to be observant and adapt to the evidence around them. Don't have the spaces between the decoys too tight – leave a bit of space for the live ones to land and feel safe in doing so. You want the decoys to signal the presence of good feeding on the ground so that the incoming woodpigeons see it and join the party.

There are a few tricks that appear to be helpful when decoying woodpigeons. One thing to watch for is to ensure that your decoys are generally facing into the wind. This doesn't mean facing them all in a strict regimental way into the wind, but more of a general principle, perhaps at slightly different angles, but into the direction of the wind nonetheless. Keep the wind blowing to your back, so the pigeons fly in facing you. Another neat trick is to add a crow decoy to the pattern, but if you do decide to add a crow, it is not a random process. They should be placed around 15 yards outside and away from the main pattern, and the area enclosed by it. This can help to attract woodpigeons because they know that if a crow is happy on the ground, things must be safe. However, this might also attract crows, and you could find you're hitting more crows than pigeons! If so, after a while pull the pigeon decoys and swap them out for some crow decoys. You need to read what's happening, and no two days will be the same.

When the woodpigeons come in and land, you will need to be fairly quick because they can soon learn that the decoys are fake and then fly off – perhaps within a few seconds. As you shoot more woodpigeons, use the dead ones as decoys, either by adding them to your pattern, or by replacing the plastic decoys with the real thing, but again, do not overcrowd the area. Your hide will need to be excellent, concealed in a tree line or thick bushes, giving almost all-round coverage. If you can spot your own hide from the field or decoy area, then you can be sure that the woodpigeon can, too, and the whole exercise is futile. Get to your hide well before the feeding times you have already established by prior research; get into place, and sit and wait.

USE A BROKEN RHYTHM

The late martial arts expert, Bruce Lee, discussed at length the need to use a broken rhythm in combat fighting. What he really meant by this was, not to use a patterned, routine and predictable approach. Be unpredictable and you'll have the speed advantage. Your opponent will not know what you're going to do next, and this will freeze them up to some extent and give you the edge. So, don't do the same thing, over and over again, or else you'll become predictable and your opponent can strategise a counter-attack. Metaphorically speaking, this idea has an application to hunting and particularly with hunting with airguns when we typically get close to our quarry.

HUNTING: FIELDCRAFT

No matter which animal is the focus of your attention, be sure to use a varied and diverse approach to keep them guessing – or at the very least, not always associating you, or what you're doing, as a threat. Animals are quick-learning and spot patterns or associations very easily, even though they obviously don't have a full understanding of them. All wild animals will have a degree of hard-wired 'skittishness' about them – they are, after all, wild. However, in addition to this will be a series of complementary behaviours and awareness from growing up in that specific micro-environment, and the hunter needs to observe and learn these. Let's explore some examples to illustrate the concept of a broken rhythm as applied to hunting.

If you always enter a field at the same entry point, at the same time of day, making the same noises, and walk in the same direction, you're becoming predictable by the quarry that might be watching, even if you cannot see them. Similarly, if you lamp the same field consecutively, night after night, by about the fourth night, some of the rabbits will have sussed out that this bright light is associated with a threat, and you have become predictable to them. Even under these circumstances, you might bag the odd, less-observant bunny, but on the whole your success will start to curtail and they will adapt.

Some people will tell you that in these situations the animals 'remember' what's going on, or grow wise to your methods. I don't think that's the best way to view it because you can return to these strategies after a short break and enjoy similar levels of success that you had at the beginning. Doesn't sound much like a memory to me. In reality, small mammals and birds learn what I'd call 'short-term contingencies', but these are quickly over-written if the hunter switches tactics. It's certainly true that an old rabbit might be harder to stalk than a juvenile, but let us be serious, a rabbit has a brain the size of a walnut and it needs to feed and breed just as much as anything else does. Therefore, even an old wise rabbit should not pose too much of a problem to a serious hunter who should have a variety of methods, approaches and techniques at their disposal.

If you feel you cannot stalk a given rabbit because you keep spooking it, then why stalk it at all? Why not ambush it? Why not lamp it? What about night-vision? Why not sit and wait for it to come to you? It most certainly will if you've done your research and placed yourself correctly. Why not just sit and wait? Or, just lay off those rabbits for a week or two and then come back. Trust me, all will be forgotten. In that time period, chances are they've been running from raptors and foxes every day and night. You're old history.

The crucial point here is not to become so predictable that the rabbit – or any species – alters its short-term behaviour. You need to use a 'broken rhythm', a non-predictable approach. Some days, make sure you're there; some nights be there; sometimes stalk, use different stalking directions at different times, use different entry points into the space; sometimes ambush and get into position early; sometimes add camo-netting or hides to aid concealment in new places; sometimes lamp; sometimes use night-vision, if you can; sometimes sit and wait for them to come to you. Sometimes leave an area undisturbed for a few days or a week or two ... use all these methods, mixed up and for different durations. Remember, your brain is bigger than a walnut, but you've still got to use it! This is a crucial part of the fieldcraft of modern hunting with airguns. Some might think I'm over-complicating things here, and argue to pick up the gun and just go hunting, and you might enjoy limited success with that attitude, but if you're serious about offering a service to landowners and farmers, then you need to return that trust by offering optimal solutions. People might bring a couple of rabbits home, arguing that their approach is working, but how do you know that they could not have brought 10 rabbits home? – perhaps more, had they employed these strategies. Some people say that quarry, like rabbits, are clever. Indeed they are, but in a very narrow sense. Once the hunter starts to get a feel for that 'cleverness' and its limitations, then the gap between bunny and hunter reduces.

HANDLING CULLED ANIMALS

Once an animal has been culled, there are a few things to do in the field before moving on in your shoot. For example, I always pee and paunch my rabbits in the field shortly after shooting them – within 20 minutes or so, and certainly no later than an hour in the summer. The innards can swell and heat up, ruining the meat, so it is important to paunch them fairly soon after shooting them, and even more so in very hot weather. Using your thumbs, press firmly on the tummy area of the rabbit and slide down toward the inside of the hind legs and any remaining urine in the rabbit should come out.

Once done, paunch and gut the rabbit. This can be done quickly in the field with little mess. Take your hunting knife. Pinch the fur and skin in the central stomach area, and lift the pinched area, then cut across this pinched area between your fingers

HUNTING: FIELDCRAFT

and the rabbit. Make sure not to pierce the intestines directly. The desired result is a small hole in the fur and inner skin so that the intestines are now exposed, but not pierced. Then, using your thumbs and fingers, rip open the incised hole so that it tears up and down the central body region. Get your hands in behind the upper innards, and put the lungs etc, gently away from their fixed position, but still leaving the innards in the animal. Then, hold the front legs in one hand, the rear in another, and flick or rotate the animal so that all its innards project out under the momentum of the rotation and everything should come out – aim them into a bush or undergrowth – then simply remove the poo tract, pierce the upper cavity and remove the heart and, for this part of the process, that's it. I leave them with the skin on in the field to protect the meat, and then skin them at home.

One small additional point is worth making here: it is good practice to inspect the dead rabbit for the presence of parasites. Tapeworms and tapeworm cysts can occur, so when gutting a rabbit check for them, they are often clear to see. Cysts look like small white beads and can be located between the skin and meat, and around the bowel area of the rabbit. If I encounter these I do not eat the rabbit, but use it for baiting. Some hunters argue that any microscopic parasites would be killed in the cooking process, and so as long as the animal is well cooked, it's not a problem. Perhaps, but once you can see these things they are no longer microscopic and I don't recommend eating anything where you have doubt. For years, I have always paunched rabbits with my bare hands and washed them afterwards with bottled water. I've never encountered a problem with this method, but these days I wear disposable latex gloves to ensure, as much as I can, that parasitic critters don't find their way on to me.

Finally, I thread the legs and hang the rabbits on a fence or branch for an hour or so to allow the fleas to fall off, and as a handy way to store them temporarily. To do this, make a small incision in one of the back legs, between the main leg and tendon, making sure not to cut into the meat of the leg. Hold one leg inside of the fence wire, the other leg on the other side and then thread one foot through the incision you've just made and allow to hang on the fence. Leave to hang and don't forget where it is! When hanging, pick a place out of view and that is hard to access by foxes and badgers.

For woodpigeon or collared dove that I intend to eat, I simply place them in a quarry container, which also doubles up as a shooting seat. The important thing here is to keep the flies off them so they are best kept out of the way. I'm only interested in the breast meat on these birds, so there is no need to pluck all the feathers, just those around the breast area so you can see what you're doing to get at the breast meat. Other species can be disposed of by simply throwing into nearby overgrowth or ditches, although be careful not to block the flow of any waterways or drainage running through the area. Never pick up dead rats, not even with your hunting gloves on. Use a shovel or a branch or something to move them. Dead corvids (crows, rooks, magpies) can be kept and frozen to be used on future decoying trips, and hanging dead corvids upside down from branches can act as a deterrent for its comrades and make them think twice about entering that area.

7 Hunting: Fur

RABBITS, GREY SQUIRREL, WILD MINK, RATS

Rabbits

As cute-looking as they are, rabbits are a pest species and with good reason. Rabbits eat planted crops, young tree saplings, make holes in lawns, and burrow their warrens into the landscape, which can cause subsidence or collapse. Rabbits will eat a variety of farmed crops including; potatoes, barley, wheat, carrots and turnips, and it has been estimated that they cause around £100 million worth of damage to crops every year, and so are a species that requires controlling. They take the grazing from other livestock including sheep, cows, and horses; collapsed warrens and tunnels underneath horse paddocks can potentially cause horses to break their legs or throw a rider; some forestry workers have told me that rabbits often nibble away at tree bark – known as 'ring-barking' – so that most, or even all of the bark is stripped from the tree. If the circumference of the tree is stripped, then the tree will die because nutrients from the ground cannot be fed further up. If part of the bark is stripped then the tree can be seriously compromised and although still alive, can become unstable.

Rabbits are a favoured quarry amongst hunters. Not only is one removing a pest, but they are also very tasty and an excellent source of meat and protein. They are by far my favourite meat, and there are few culinary delights to rival a well-made rabbit stew or pie. Rabbits live

A bunny tucking into the lawn of my cottage. For me, they are the tastiest of all the pest species we shoot, followed closely by the woodpigeon.

communally and like to build warrens in soft, sandy soil that can be dug and worked easily. Hedgerows, fields with shallow-rooted gorse bushes, and some woodland are ideal, and places where the soil has been disturbed, such as landfill sites, or where soil has been used to cover demolished buildings, are also suitable habitats. Close to where my father lived in the Lake District is a small hilly mound that was covered with lots of soil about 30 years ago, to hide brick rubble. It was planted with conifers on the very top of this mound, and gorse bushes at mid- and lower levels, and these evergreen gorse bushes provide an ideal habitat for what appears to be, in this case, a veritable colony of rabbits. The land is owned by Her Majesty's Government, and these rabbits are not hunted – well, not by humans, although the buzzards are ever-present. It is a good example of the type of terrain and soil favoured by the humble bunny.

Rabbits like to feed on open grassy areas where they can get their fill and see potential predators in the distance. Dense cover would make them vulnerable because predators could use this to get close to them. They will often eat far from the safety of their warrens, many hundreds of yards in search of food, and even more so at night. Surprisingly, rabbits can climb a short distance and can even swim if they have to, in order to lose a chasing predator. They start breeding from January all the way through to mid-summer, and can have an average of five to seven litters a season, each litter containing around five kittens, and some have suggested that a litter of 12 kittens is not unprecedented.

When shooting rabbits, it is important to think about whether the goal is to eradicate all numbers because the landowner wants them all gone – i.e., pest control; to control the numbers and keep them to a healthy minimum – a land-management approach; or whether you are just shooting a few bunnies for the pot to eat.

For pest control, it is legitimate to shoot rabbits all year round and even if you do shoot a pregnant rabbit, from this perspective some hunters argue it's a good thing because you have taken out a number of rabbits with one single shot, and I cannot argue with the maths. From a land-management perspective, one might leave rabbits alone earlier in the year when their breeding season starts, make inroads into them later on and just take the mature ones. If you are only interested in a few bunnies for the pot, then leave them until later in the year when the first young will be maturing and soon be good to eat.

As I've grown older, and arguably softer, I prefer the land-management approach, but will of course, seek to implement the wishes of the landowner. Personally, I actually

HUNTING: FUR

do like to see rabbits running wild, but not in high numbers. In most scenarios, I leave the tiddlers and concentrate on the more mature ones, but rabbits breed … well … like rabbits, and a small number of them can soon become a problem if things are not kept in check. If you are going to be more relaxed about your rabbit shooting, it is important not to be so relaxed that it becomes a problem for the landowner. If they are causing a problem and the landowner wants them gone, then hit them hard. Otherwise, develop an approach that is effective, sporting, and fair.

Good rabbit shooting can be had in the fading light of the evening, the dead of night, and the early morning, and in situations where there are no immediate predators, or they are not being bothered by humans, they will be out and about even in the midday sun. While there are certainly some commonalities, in general rabbit behaviour there are some important differences across locations as well. If rabbits have been well hunted, by humans or other predators, then their general behaviour will be very skittish. In contrast, if rabbits are fairly used to seeing humans at a distance, and have no major predators in the immediate region, then they will be more relaxed about things.

I would never describe the latter scenario as the rabbits being 'tame', but their flight responses will have adapted to their immediate situation. For example, the rabbits found on a golf course tend to behave differently to the presence of humans than those found in wild fields and woods. Over the years, I have hunted on land where rabbits have shown both extremes of behaviour. When gaining a new rabbit shooting permission, it is important to establish their behavioural patterns before hitting them. Rabbits learn fast, so even if your first few forays are easy pickings, that will not last. You want to ensure that your initial impact on the numbers is as maximal as it can be, in order to get on top of the problem as soon as possible – so do your research.

It is a good idea not to be tempted to shoot rabbits as soon as they emerge from their warrens. Wait a short while because you will often see more and more rabbits emerge, and they might split up a little in the field as they settle down. The hunter, with a fully moderated airgun, might well be able to pick off separate bunnies without spooking any of the others, thus increasing the number bagged relative to what one would have gleaned if we were overly hasty. Be patient.

Rabbits are not the hardest animal to shoot, but that does not mean they are easy, either. Relative to say woodpigeon and crows, shooting rabbits can be more straightforward. A variety of approaches work well including; stalking, ambushing, night-vision and lamping. It is a common view that rabbits have poor vision, but this is not strictly accurate. Rabbits can actually see with an almost 360º field of view, athough they have a blind spot directly in front of the face. A rabbit's visual system has evolved for foraging and for the quick, effective detection of approaching predators from many directions; i.e., raptors from the skies, as well as foxes from the ground. Rabbits are thought to be far-sighted which helps with detecting those airborne and more distant threats. However, the central blind spot in the rabbit's field of view prevents a clear, three-dimensional view of nearby objects, and they do not share our level of depth perception at close range. Rabbits can see a few colours to some degree, most notably those we see as blue and green, but they cannot see red and orange colours. They have a high visual sensitivity in low light conditions, and they well perceive movement or lights, but they have a poor level of visual acuity, meaning that although they can detect a change in their environment, which might signal a predator via biological motion, they will not be able to see much visual detail of the threat. Knowledge about how animals see and experience the world provides the hunter with a more comprehensive understanding of its behaviour, and how to adapt the situation to their advantage.

In woodland, rabbits will often run from the warrens and through the thicket until they reach a nearby clearing before stopping to feed. This is likely due to the fact that they feel safer when out of the dense foliage where predators can be lurking. Once you've located warrens surrounded by dense brambles, saplings, trees, and so on, look for a nearby grassy clearing because the chances are, when they emerge that is where they will bolt for – the presence of scratchings and droppings will confirm this. It is not an exact science, but I've seen it often enough to have capitalised on it more times than I can remember. The clearing becomes the kill space; the hunter places themselves in or near to the dense thicket or foliage so not to be detected.

Although never an argument you will encounter from the anti-shooting groups, I genuinely believe that the rabbit population itself benefits if it is managed by hunting enthusiasts. Let me explain: Myxomatosis is a truly horrible disease that affects rabbits and in most cases is fatal. Now, over the last decade or so I have never encountered a single case of myxomatosis on any of my rabbit-shooting land. However, it has been spotted a number of times within one and a half miles distance from me, on land that is not being shot over, and in some nearby parts of the Lake District it has completely annihilated the local rabbit population with little or no recovery in those regions.

HUNTING: FUR

To my mind, these observations support the notion that if the population of rabbits in a given area is not allowed to get out of control, and maintained at a small but manageable level, then they are far less vulnerable to fatal infections and diseases. This is because if a given rabbit population cannot come into close contact with an infected population, then the chances of transmission are minimised to the betterment of the rabbit population you are managing. Myxomatosis is a hideous disease, leading to the protracted and inhumane demise of the rabbit. When and where it is observed in the wild, the most humane approach is the lethal and instantaneous removal of the animal. It is not an exact science because flying insects that could cover some distance, as well as fleas, can transmit myxomatosis, but I am of the opinion that controlling rabbit numbers reduces the opportunity of transmission. Put simply, areas I know of that have a shooting-based conservation project in place, still have healthy rabbits present. A lot of the areas I know of that are not being managed have few, if any rabbits because, at some point, myxomatosis has already wiped them out.

More recently, there has been the emergence of Rabbit Haemorrhagic Disease (RHD and its variant RHD-2), a highly infectious and largely fatal virus that attacks the respiratory system and lungs of the rabbit, and it is being held responsible for a noticeable drop in rabbit numbers around the world. RHD is more of an invisible killer, with few visible signs in the wild rabbit population, and most will die out of sight, deep in their warrens after having descended into a coma some hours earlier. Thankfully, there is some evidence that rabbits are now developing some resistance to myxomatosis, although it is too early to tell if the same is occurring for RHD, which at the time of writing, appears to be a serious problem for the wild rabbit population.

One good reason not to put a squirrel feeder near to the ground! This little bunny came and sat in the feeder daily whilst it remained small enough to do so.

GREY SQUIRREL

Grey squirrels are pests and require culling for a variety of reasons. They strip the bark on trees and damage growing shoots, costing millions annually to the forestry industry. Grey squirrels are omnivores, so as well as eating fruit, nuts, vegetation, and shrubs, they raid the nests of certain songbirds, and eat the eggs or the young. They also drive out our native endangered red squirrel. Grey squirrels can carry parapoxvirus, known as 'squirrel pox', although they are not affected by it. In contrast, it is deadly for the red squirrel, who can contract the virus and die within 10 days. Recent studies have also suggested that a percentage of grey squirrels also carry the ticks that host the Borrelia species of bacteria that causes Lyme disease, and a bite from an infected tick can be responsible for the transmission to humans. There are four types of bacteria that can be carried by ticks and cause Lyme disease, and all can be carried by grey squirrels, although certain regions might be associated with one particular type of the bacteria. Grey squirrels are also a problem in urban environments. There are cases of them getting inside the roof spaces or lofts of domestic dwellings, and inside churches, causing thousands of pounds worth of damage, and setting fires through chewing wires, as well.

The infamous grey squirrel. They might look cute, but they are a serious problem in both rural and urban areas.

Greys have twice the body mass of the native endangered red squirrel. They can have two litters a year, typically January through to May, with between two and six kits per-litter. They like favourable weather and are rarely out in torrential downpours or the severe cold, but they do not hibernate in the winter, although they become less active in the deep winter months, emerging only to forage for hidden caches of food, and then returning to the safety and

HUNTING: FUR

warmth of their dreys for several days. You can see them out and about between snow showers, for example, when with thick cloud cover it can be warmer than you think, and the shooting can be good, but on the whole their activity is somewhat reduced during this time.

Grey squirrels are clever; a single animal can have many dreys – three on average – one of which will be specific for birthing, the others work as a back-up in case some get raided, taken over, damaged by weather, or attacked by predators. Some dreys can be used on different nights as the squirrel forages through the outer reaches of its home range, before returning to its main drey of use. There are no known differences between a red or grey squirrel drey. In some ways, dreys might seem similar to magpie nests in that both are basically nests with a roof on. True, but there are important differences to to be aware of if you go drey-spotting. For example, a squirrel drey is located in the upper third of the tree, not the top, and tightly packed, typically wedged in the 'V' space of an upward branch stemming from the central tree trunk. A drey can be made of twigs with leaves still attached, and can consist of a variety of additional materials like sheep wool, pine needles and moss. Dreys can also be made

I see you! Squirrel dreys revealed in the winter woodland. Dreys are distinctive in that they tend to be built in the last third or so of the tree, in a 'V' section between the central trunk and a sturdy branch, and they consist of a mix of materials like twigs, leaves, sheep wool, moss, etc. Locating dreys is very useful for informing your squirrel culling strategy. The depths of winter is the best time to go drey spotting when there are few leaves on the trees and they become more exposed.

inside tree holes made by fallen branches. In contrast, magpie nests are located at the tops of trees high in the canopy and consist of clean twigs – no moss, wool, etc. Once you become aware of these differences, you'll never confuse the two.

Grey squirrels adapt well to their environments, a factor that clearly contributes to their growing numbers. They engage in making fake food caches, in case they are being watched by other squirrels, and have their favourite feeding places and well-established routes to and from their multiple dreys. This means that their behaviour can be predicted and with a bit of research in the area, this can also be used to establish a location for your own feeder, to ambush.

Squirrel feeding behaviour follows what is known as the 'Optimal Foraging Theory' where they assess the profitability of different food types; they always prefer food that is energetically favourable, based on the nutritional content minus the energy it takes to obtain and consume the item. The more energy and calories contained within the food, the more likely it will be chosen first by the squirrel. Their feeding behaviour also changes seasonally and with what is on offer in the woodland. They will exhaust the source of the most calorific items in the woodland first, before moving on to the next best food items, and so on – and this why it is important to pay attention to your optimal feed mix that you might want to place in your squirrel feeders. The food choices of grey squirrels are also known to be mediated by the perceived risk associated with certain foods and their location.

Grey squirrels are deceptive. One might think that their humble size makes them easy to dispatch – think again! Grey squirrels are well known for being tough little buggers. The brain POI is quite small, even more so 25 yards away – and they are also fast-moving animals. These factors make them a challenging, although highly satisfying animal to shoot. To be effective at squirrel shooting with an air rifle, you need to be highly precise. It is unlikely you will get that close to them either, so being precise, at distance, is a necessary skill. Squirrel shooting can take place all year round, but in dense woodland is best in the autumn, winter or early spring months when the trees have lost their leaves. In December, grey squirrels can be seen chasing each other on the woodland floor, engaged in a kind of pre-mating ritual with the male chasing the female. It's a good time to hit them because their attention will not be on you. Mr Squirrel has romance on his mind!

Squirrels have good eyesight. Their vision is slightly biased upwards, to look for predators from the sky, but the chances are, they will see you on the ground long before you see them, or get into range, if you are stalking around the woods.

HUNTING: FUR 7

When they spot you they will often simply stop, freeze and watch you, sometimes for quite a while. On occasion, I've spotted a squirrel frozen to the spot with its head orientated toward me and watching me. It is spooked, yet highly curious. They do this more when they think that they are well covered and hidden. Look carefully through the leaves and you can see the squirrel eyeing you up, often with only its head being visible to you.

You will need to be well concealed to make effective inroads into their numbers. A lot of your squirrel hunting will involve you looking up into the trees, so it is helpful to have your face covered. Some hunters use a fine-mesh face-netting, which is effective at covering your face, but I often find it annoying when trying to look down the scope. I prefer to use either a snood pulled up over my chin, cheeks and nose, and a hat on top of my head, or a balaclava so that my face is covered, but my vision is not obscured. I also suggest covering your hands. You might not need to be so prepared for juvenile squirrels, but it is prudent to be prepared for the worst case scenario because you have no idea what will cross your path while out in the woods.

One personal observation I have made numerous times is that the hunter is not spotted so readily by grey squirrels in dull or flat lighting that might occur in the early morning, near to dusk, or on a misty or foggy day. On these occasions, I've even been standing out in the open woods and not been spotted by a squirrel running across

Looking, but not seeing.
If Mr Squirrel is leaping about the floor, try clicking your tongue. They will often stop and sit up wondering what on earth is going on. Here, I'm about 20 yards away, buried into a hedgerow and having just clicked my tongue – the squirrel has no idea where I am. You'll have enough time to squeeze a shot off providing you make no movements at this stage of high alert. He is lucky here that I was armed with a Nikon DSLR camera and not an Air Arms rifle!

the winter woodland floor. So, like many things, although it is true that squirrels have good eyesight, these factors need to be considered alongside other information, and there will certainly be instances when the squirrel will pass close by and show no interest or signs of having noticed you at all. As a side note, I've also had good rabbit shooting on days of 'flat' light, so perhaps this reflects something about mammal perception.

Occasionally, you might get close enough and spook a grey squirrel, even if you didn't see it originally. They will often run up the tree in a corkscrew fashion, but after one rotation stay on the opposite side to you. If shooting with a friend, send them around the other side of the tree and he/she will flush the squirrel back around to your side, whilst it climbs the tree, which could be enough to squeeze a shot off. You could also try throwing a stone or something similar into the undergrowth on the other side because the noise and movement might be sufficient to spook it around to your position. Alternatively, sit and wait – they often emerge higher up the tree to take a closer look at what spooked them. Remember, they are curious, and all is not lost once they are spooked; they will pause or even re-emerge in another place close by, in order to watch you. Be vigilant.

I'm pretty sure that squirrels use high trees as look-out spots. Countless times I have seen a single squirrel perched high on a relatively naked tree, surveying its environment and grooming itself. They are far out of range, but have the best view of the area. I always make a note of the trees they appear to use, at the times they use them, and try to use that information to inform my next ambush.

If hunting with airguns, by far the most effective way to hunt grey squirrels is with a feeder-based approach (see the section on hunting techniques and fieldcraft). Once you have established the best location for the feeder, and your hidden shooting position, simply fill the feeder with mix, and wait until the feed is being noticeably eaten. I suggest not shooting on a new feeder for around 8–10 days, even if the feed is being hit aggressively before this time period. Trust me, the shooting will be better if left for a short while, to allow for a greater number of grey squirrels in the area to realise that a free stash of goodies is there.

Once you have left it for a while and established when it is being hit by the squirrels – by consulting trail camera footage – try to get into position on the day of shooting 30 minutes or so beforehand, and wait to ambush them as they come in. Do not break cover when you have shot them until you are really confident that there are no more around. It is possible to shoot multiple squirrels at the same feeder,

HUNTING: FUR

in the same session, but only if you remain hidden. They are not perturbed by the presence of their culled comrades so leave them where they fall, but do ensure that your shots have been lethal and a clean kill has occurred, otherwise break cover and rectify the situation swiftly.

On a relatively still day with little or no wind, you can often hear the squirrels scurrying through the trees, approaching the feeder long before you see them. When a grey squirrel jumps from one tree canopy to another, you will hear that sound stand out from the background woodland noise and it will signal something 'large' – well, larger than the songbirds – is close by. This sound might also be accompanied by the visual spectacle of rapidly swaying branches that move with more vigour than those surrounding them being moved by the breeze alone. Even if you have not yet visually confirmed the presence of the grey squirrel, the chances are that these signs signal its presence. Get ready and set your airgun on the feeder because it will only be a few seconds before it emerges on the feeder or the tree hosting it. On many occasions, I've witnessed grey squirrels scurry down trees very close to me or even just behind me. Again, this has a distinct sound to it that you will recognise once you've heard it. Stay still if this happens. Chances are you have not been detected yet. In these circumstances the squirrel has dinner on its mind and is making its way to your feeder, which should be the optimal shooting position for it. Stick to your game plan and try not to be tempted to swing round and take a hurried shot at a squirrel that has probably now spotted you due to your movement. Patience and discipline will pay off here. You have put your feeder there for a reason – let it do its job.

WILD MINK

Wild mink are mustelids, related to weasels and stoats and all can be shot or trapped, although trapping is by far the most effective way of culling them. Most of what I am going to discuss here is related to mink, but much of it is also applicable to the smaller stoats and weasels. Mink can be found on land that is typically near water – rivers, streams, becks. In the UK, only the fox is above the mink for the accolade of apex land predator. Wild mink are fierce creatures and carry a formidable reputation. This is well known to those who live around them, but not so well known in the broader general population.

Where I grew up, there were many stories of people encountering mink around farm buildings, and it was said to be very aggressive and confident in its ability to

THE AIRGUNNER'S COMPANION

defend itself, should you stumble across one and surprise it. If cornered in a building, mink will attack and be driven to find an exit. This may mean running at and past you in its bid for freedom – which it will do without hesitation. The mink might not want confrontation, but it is very capable in such situations. Once established in an area, mink are very territorial and ferociously defend their habitat against other mink, so sightings of them will be rare. As a consequence you cannot really 'hunt' or stalk mink because they are far too elusive.

Within the scope of their territory, mink might have several dens, including old rabbit warrens and burrows in river banks. Wild mink are carnivores with a tremendously strong bite and sharp teeth and will eat anything they can kill. Unlike a fox, they will attack and kill animals many times their own size; rats, water voles, young rabbits, ground-nesting birds, wildfowl, some game and poultry, and they fish the rivers for crayfish, eels and bigger species of fish.

Mink raid songbird nests for eggs and fledgling birds, and like foxes, if they get inside a hen house containing lots of small animals, they will not stop until they have killed all of them because they are excited and triggered by the movement of living animals – not necessarily the size of their appetite. Thus, they kill even when they are not hungry. In some ways, they can be more of a problem than foxes because they can climb fencing and trees effectively, and so extra efforts are needed to make poultry pens mink-proof. It is thought that similar behaviour occurs if they stumble across fish pools in rivers and streams – they will kill everything in sight, if they can, taking only a few bites out of each fish before moving on to the next one. In recent years mink have also been attributed with raiding garden and domestic ponds for expensive fish and other wildlife. The only reason mink are not more of a problem in the countryside is due to their solitary nature so there will never be a group of them in one given area. Stoats, and to a lesser extent the smaller weasel, also take rabbits and small rodents for food, but although legal to shoot, they are simply too fast!

I've heard some hunters say that because wild mink are extremely good 'ratters', perhaps it is a good idea to leave them alone and have them as allies on your broader approach to land management, but I do not concur. Mink will kill rats when they encounter them, but they also kill fish, sometimes emptying entire pools of young fish, which could make rivers barren over time; they also attack and kill small poultry, costing farmers considerable money, and mink will always prefer the easy pickings of a songbird nest over fighting a rat. To my mind, the negatives outweigh the positives, if indeed you accept that there are any positives. In my opinion, if you encounter wild mink, dispatch them immediately.

Because they are elusive and territorial, mink sightings are rare and there might only ever be one – or a mating pair – on the land you shoot, if they are there at all. You will not encounter many of them over your shooting life, so it is an experience to value when it happens. I don't know why, but by weird coincidence I have encountered mink in the wild a few times – all by chance and never by design. I haven't gone out specifically to hunt them because encounters are unpredictable, and they are so elusive. I've simply been in the right place at the right time. In over 35 years of shooting, I've seen three wild mink, shot at two, completely missed one, and killed just one of them. The one I did shoot was killed instantly with a head shot, from about 25 yards, on a farm with a rat problem. If it was there because the rats were, then it was not good at keeping the rat numbers down at all, so I'm not convinced by the 'effective ratters' argument.

I have been asked whether an air rifle can kill a mink. I can assure the reader that a sub-12 ft.lbs. airgun is more than suitable for controlling mink – with clean head shots, stone dead, no problem. Their skulls are not thick at all and they pose no challenge to a hunter who is precise with an airgun. At the start of this book I mentioned this mink shot; it is one that I will always remember and a story I'd like to share. I was about 17 years old and had been shooting on farm land with a friend that day, with little success. I had my HW80 with me, which was still fairly new, and my good friend and shooting buddy had his Theoben Sirocco, again fairly new. We were walking back toward the farmhouse on a midsummer afternoon when I spotted a shiny, black 'creature' crawling up a thick branch on a fallen tree on the opposite side of the track to the farmhouse. The branch was about six feet from the ground, and roughly parallel with some minor elevation. The animal was moving slowly along the branch and was around head height when it stopped. It was fairly relaxed and in no rush to go anywhere on this summer evening.

I stopped in my tracks and quietly shouted, 'Oi' to my friend who was a couple of yards behind and to the right of me. I was standing about 25 yards away from the animal, and shouldered my gun to take a better look through the scope. At this point, I thought it might have been a cat, but at the same time knew something was very odd about the way it was moving. Through the scope I could see a wet, shiny and dark creature, but its head was like that of a ferret, so I knew it wasn't a cat, and then it dawned on me that it was a mink.

As I'd spotted it first, the shot was mine – those were the rules between us – so I placed the crosshairs directly on its head, just behind the eye. Knowing full well the stories and legends of such predators, I squeezed off a very nervous shot, the .22 pellet hit home with an audible 'thwack', and the mink was sent flying from the tree. I could tell by the way it fell that it was a clean kill and dead, but knowing the reputation of the mink, I quickly reloaded in case it was annoyed, and then slowly and somewhat gingerly approached the tree from where it had fallen. Sure enough, there it was belly up in the grass, stone dead. I received a pat on the back from my shooting buddy and we showed the farmer – he was well pleased. It would be many years until I saw another mink. Although by no means the most challenging shot I have ever taken, it was a mink, a pest of some reputation and I was young and learning these skills, so it was a very satisfying experience and one I remember clearly to this day.

Rats

For me, wild brown rats are the only animal I would quite happily shoot into complete extinction if I could. They have no redeeming features. Rats are pests and for good reason. They carry many diseases, including Weil's syndrome, and rat-bite fever, all of which are very serious for humans. Weil's disease, also known as leptospirosis, can permanently affect the liver and kidneys, with fatal consequences in some cases. Recent floods in the UK have seen the number of cases of rat-based infections increase, due to rat pee being present in the flood water and now reaching a wider area due to the flood. Rats wee and poo as they run around, so their bodies and fur are coated in the stuff, and hence also coated in bacteria and disease. Rat bites can also cause tetanus infections. For these reasons, never handle a dead rat – not even by the tail. Rats also eat when the food is in the field, stored on the farm, or even in the supermarket or store. Such infestations mean they infect the food through their droppings and wee, all of which can cost thousands of pounds to the food industry and farmers. They can also gnaw through structures – woodwork and electrical – causing extensive damage.

Some farmland that I shoot on has been riddled with rats, and others completely clear of them, and I've often wondered why. The presence of rivers and becks is certainly one factor. It is the case that some farmers have cleaner practices than others, and so food is not as readily available for the rats, but I also note that famers who have terrier dogs roaming on their land also have very few, if any, rats. The Jack Russell terrier is a formidable ratter and I've never seen a large rat problem where these dogs rule the area.

In rural areas, whenever possible I will avoid using poisons to eliminate rats. This is mainly because other species – dogs, cats, raptors – can take the poison, become ill or die. Even if the poison itself is well concealed, anything feeding on the dead rat carcass could potentially become poisoned themselves, so it's hardly a precise exercise. This is also where the airgun can come into its own as a highly effective tool for controlling the rat population.

Rat shooting can be great sport. They are fast-moving and are often present in such large numbers that the floor can move with them on occasion. They can jump high into the air when shot, and the remaining rats will feed on the blood and even the carcass (cannibalism) if really hungry. They are grim creatures and shooting them is not for the faint-hearted. You need to go into their domain and get close.

In the summer months, rats can be found out in open fields and on river banks, although they're often too well hidden, or too fast to shoot. In the winter months they tend to head for the warmth of outbuildings and the feed or seed stores in sheds on the farm. Rats are much easier to shoot around farm buildings because the concrete floors provide no hiding place or coverage, so they are fully exposed. However, rats are not just floor creatures. They can scurry through and up the walls and along wooden roof beams and rafters. The first step in rat shooting is to establish where on the farm they are. Sacks of seed, or feed with signs of gnawed edges, the presence of droppings, etc should help to give away their preferred locations. They are active at most times, but rat-shooting is generally a nocturnal or dusk activity, and every situation is different. If there are no dogs around and they are generally undisturbed, rats will be plentiful during the day, but if there is a lot of activity in the area, ratty will prefer evening forays around the food sheds. Although you will always be able to pop the odd few opportunistically, by wandering around, the most effective way to make a big impact on numbers is a well-planned ambush.

Assuming that the research has been done, pick a spot from which to sit and ambush. Good concealment is still important; hide behind anything available – straw bales, machinery, etc. Make sure you have an excellent view of the kill zone and that it is a safe area to shoot into. Is the pellet safe if you miss? I'd recommend a shooting distance of around 15 yards – not much more for such a small and fast-moving target. Take a portable shooting seat if needs be. A shooting stick is also helpful. If you're using lamping as a method and if the barn has lights, turn one of them on, but nothing too bright. Ideally, you should have left the dim lights on for a few nights previously, so that they get used to it. You don't need the place lit up like daylight because this will scare them off, but just enough to illuminate the area. Then, sit and wait.

It is possible to lamp rats, or shoot them under a dim light, but night-vision has taken rat-shooting to a whole new level. You can sit there all night popping away at them and they have no idea where you are. To help boost your chances of success, bait an area with food for them. Do this for a few days before you plan to hit them. Then, on the final day, be there and be ready. Coupled to night-vision or lamping, it is a deadly method.

A word on shooting around farm buildings. It is always of paramount importance to ensure that with any shot, should you miss, the pellet travels to a safe place. It is important to consider ricochets and that no damage can happen to the building. I've known some hunters shoot out roof tiles and glass windows due to missing the target, ricochets, and over-penetration when the pellet has gone straight through the animal and on into the asbestos roof tile – not good. Extra care is needed when shooting around farm buildings. It is also vital to have a good appreciation of where people could emerge from and enter your shooting area. Always be prepared for people – and indeed some animals – straying into the area, unaware that you are there.

8 Hunting: Feather

WOODPIGEON, COLLARED DOVES, FERAL PIGEON, CORVIDS – MAGPIES, CROWS, ROOKS, JACKDAWS, BLUE-JAYS.

It is worth noting that any potential shooting of pest bird species is assessed relative to the general licences, and that all criteria have been satisfied in regard to the use of lethal methods. Rather than repeat this for each species throughout this section, all the information discussed below should be viewed in the context that this important step has been considered and the terms and conditions of the licences satisfied.

Woodpigeons

Woodpigeons are wary creatures. It is unlikely you will just stumble across one and get the time to shoulder the gun and pull a considered shot off. By the time you stumble across them, there will be a flurry of clapping wings and they're gone! So if woodies are on the agenda, a more strategic approach is necessary. Like rabbit, woodpigeon is not only a pest species, but also very tasty. A head or throat shot from an air rifle means that all the meat will be undisturbed, and can be used for the pot. You will never go back to chicken once you've tried woodpigeon!

Shotgunners are masters at shooting the woodpigeon because they can shoot them when the bird is in full flight, as well as perched in sitty trees and decoyed onto the ground. The airgunner cannot shoot woodpigeon when they are in flight. Nevertheless, the airgun is an extremely effective tool for shooting woodpigeon when coupled to certain techniques. Hunting woodies with airguns typically means hide-shooting, decoying them to the ground, or ambushing their sitty trees. The idea in these scenarios is to get the woodpigeon stationary, so it can be shot.

Although rare, it is possible to shoot more than one woodpigeon from a collection of them, with a moderated air rifle and I have experienced this myself on some occasions. In a sitty tree, the woodies will disperse themselves at various levels in the tree. In reasonable, although not excessive winds, I have shot woodpigeons on the lower branches, without the rest of them higher up flying off. The shot woodpigeons were lower in the tree (relative to the others), so the remaining ones might not see it fall, and the wind can mask the noise of the woodpigeon falling, or they might think the bird is flying down to the ground to feed, as opposed to dropping to the ground stone dead. I've no idea, but I have done it more than once. Sometimes it works, sometimes it's a complete failure. A moderated air rifle is also a big help here, but the noise of impact from the pellet hitting the animal is often enough to spook the others, although not always. If such an opportunity presents itself to you, give it a try.

You can target woodies out in the fields when they go to feed, by using a hide and decoys, or ambush them in the woods or farm buildings when they return to rest. Try to note their entry flight paths into the fields and locate their preferred sitty trees in the woods. Camouflage is a must – face and hands well covered with few if any sudden movements made. The shots themselves can be challenging for a number

Two tempting shots - which to go for? On certain occasions you could shoot both. Shoot the lower bird (in this case a magpie) first, as the higher placed woodpigeon might not see it fall. In reasonable winds, they might not hear it fall either. Such situations are rare, but if they do present themselves always try to hit the one that is lowest first. The magpie would certainly see the pigeon drop in front of it if the pigeon was the first shot. Obviously, a fully moderated air rifle would be needed to pull this off. Be prepared for more failure than success, but success can be had in the right conditions. If a situation like this presents itself to you, give it a try.

HUNTING: FEATHER

of reasons; the angle of the shot might be steep so you'll need to compensate for the degree of incline from your shooting position – aim lower. If you spook one, chances are they will all scarper, although they often return a few minutes later so sit tight. When roosting or sitting in trees after feeding, woodies will often be motionless whilst having what appears to be a nice well-earned nap. That's a good time to hit them because their alertness is lowered and their heads and throats are still, so let them come into the trees, land and settle for a few minutes. In contrast, if you've decoyed them into a kill space on the ground, you will need to shoot them within a few seconds after they have landed, and before they have realised the decoys are fake. Be quick!

COLLARED DOVES

Collared dove shooting can be at its best around the farmyard. Collared doves are not quite as skittish as the woodpigeon and are often found in pairs, and like the rabbit and woodpigeon, as well as being a pest they are very tasty. They like feeding on harvested grains around farmyards and you can get quite close to them before they fly off. When they are outside and around the farmyard, they are often perched on rooftops, pylon wires and fence posts – anything that gives them a good view of the area, before dropping to the ground to feed. They are used to seeing people about on the farm and are not threatened by the presence of humans at reasonable distances, so you can take your time with the shot and compose yourself. They are often unperturbed by your presence, providing you are no closer than 20–25 yards, so you don't really need to decoy them, or anything of that nature – well, not around the farmyard. It is simply unnecessary in this situation.

Inside the barns and grain store, they like the height of the rafters or roof beams to snuggle into, between their own forays to the ground. During the late summer months, place yourself in the barn or building that is storing the grain. Make sure that you are hidden using what is available – any nearby bales of straw or hay, machinery, pallets of wood etc. – as an impromptu hide. You could be in for some good shooting, even more so if they know not to fear you.

Alternatively, a considered walk around the farm is often all that is needed to spot and take them. Keep movements slow and quiet and you should be OK. I would suggest not hitting them too regularly because they will become hard to get close to over time, by way of the setting up of short-term contingencies when they associate your specific presence as being a threat. Therefore, do have dedicated days for shooting them and make it count as much as possible because it's a good idea then to leave them for a while. If they are a problem on the land you are shooting over, take them when you can. They can become a problem in high numbers and most farmers want them gone due to the damage they do in the grain sheds.

FERAL PIGEONS

Shooting feral pigeons is much the same as that described above for collared doves. I find that these birds also like the farmyard and outbuildings a lot for their easy pickings. Again, there is little need for hide-building and decoys, although adding the odd pigeon or magpie decoy to a fence post, water trough or similar can make them settle in the area a little quicker. Keep a reasonable distance and try to use the farmyard to aid concealment, but feral pigeons are much more forgiving than the woodpigeon for the same reasons as collared doves. They seem to be fairly unperturbed by the presence of humans – at least to some degree. The best way to target feral pigeons is to simply observe what building and areas they like to perch in. Use items around the farm – like pallets or something – to hide behind and wait for them to come back in. They will, so be ready.

CORVIDS

BLUE-JAYS

The beautiful blue-jay is part of the corvid family and also a pest because they are known to raid the nests of songbirds and eat the eggs or young chicks. I have spoken to gamekeepers and woodsmen who argue that jays are much worse than magpies for raiding nests, and they ask that I dispatch them at all times, but I must confess, I rarely shoot jays these days. To be honest, I see far too few of them, so on the whole, I'll leave them alone. If they are raiding nests, they seem to be so rare on the land I shoot that I really doubt the impact on the songbird population.

Jays are elusive and you are most likely to encounter them in deep woodland. They tend to be in pairs and I've seen a few couples flying and dancing through the tree canopy of hardwood woodlands. Like other corvids (magpies, rooks, crows) they are very clever and I have also seen them around the squirrel feeder picking up seeds the squirrel is dropping, so they know when to fly in and capitalise on a situation. They can be difficult to target. If you've seen them once in a place, you will see them again, so you can predict your encounters at least to some degree. Shooting jays tends to be more of a chance-encounter thing than the result of any a priori strategy. If jays are a problem on the land you shoot, they can be a satisfying quarry due to their elusiveness, but if they're not causing any discernible problem, and are rare, I'd leave them – although keep an eye on things in case the decision needs to be reversed.

Magpies

Magpies are the hooligans of the sky and often travel in gangs; they attack songbirds, raid their nests and take over other bird nests as their own, and they are territorial, very clever, and a worthy adversary for the shooter, but they have excellent eyesight and learn very fast. They can also be aggressive towards other birds or animals – I've seen them try to dive-bomb and harass young grey squirrels perched on feeders.

Like all corvids, they have an inquisitive nature. Shortly after I purchased my first PCP, I shot six magpies in a row in under a minute, and the success was all down to the shooting of the first one, which acted as a kind of decoy resembling one that appeared to be in distress. The bird was not in any distress, it was dead, but its posture on the ground seemed very attractive to the other birds. Once the first magpie rolled over and spread it wings, its comrades came flying in to mob it and assess what was wrong. They made a tremendous noise clucking away as more and more flew in, landed, and walked straight up to it. I quickly popped the second, chambered another pellet, and popped the third, and so on. The more I shot, the more noisy, almost deafening bewilderment ensued, until the number of birds contributing to the noise began to reduce significantly. The moderated airgun kept my position concealed and the multi-shot PCP ensured a fast reload. What started out as an opportunistic shot on one magpie quickly became a corvid apocalypse!

Since this experience I often place the first dead magpie into a distressed-looking position, belly up with its wings – or one of them – pegged out. The dead bird works as a decoy in most situations, but these types of postures appear to be particularly effective at getting them interested. I have also attached fishing line to one of the wings of a dead magpie and gone back to my hide to pull on the other end of the line, to simulate twitching/movement in the wing. This can be very effective at luring any nearby gang in because their curiosity gets the better of them.

The inquisitive nature of the magpie can often be its undoing and the hunter can use this to great effect. Magpies like to investigate things and this means they can be decoyed into an area. An opened up squirrel or rabbit, with the innards lying out, coupled to a magpie decoy works well. Place these items in the field, or an open area where they can be seen, and take cover in a nearby and convincing hide. Again, once they fly in and you shoot one, the others will tend to come. Be careful – they are very aware of their surroundings so you will need to be in position and concealed at all times. In more urban settings, try a bin liner ripped open and full of food waste. If you see them coming in, get your gun into your shoulder before they land on the ground because your movement will be easier for them to see when they are stationary on the ground.

My father taught me a neat trick, which is well known and has been written about a great deal in hunting literature. You can 'call' magpies towards you by shaking a half-full box of matches, which when done at an appropriate frequency and intensity can mimic the magpie call. I use the large box of Chef's matches to get a good noise of a similar tone – a deeper tone from a bigger box. You just need to engage their interest and then they will often fly into range. When doing this do not reply to every call, and not always a matched number of calls – mix it up and keep them interested, then as they come into range, swap the matchbox for your gun. Shooting magpies can be very rewarding because you have to use your wits and be a good shot, but remember, they learn quickly. If you have a successful day popping them off in one

The infamous magpie, the hooligan of the skies. A highly intelligent and keen-eyed corvid. They can often be found in gangs and there can be some great shooting to be had after you've popped the first one as the others will often fly in to mob it. If you can reduce their numbers, the songbirds will be grateful.

HUNTING: FEATHER

location using a particular method, then expect neither the method nor location to be as effective next time. When it's going well, make it count.

Crows

As with magpies, crows are extremely clever corvids. They are territorial and can build more than one nest to fool predators; they can mob raptors and attack buzzards and owls, particularly around nesting time. They often work in pairs when doing this – mobbing the raptor and establishing their dominance in the region. Crows are very observant, cautious, are known to have good problem-solving skills, and even engage in tool use by using twigs and stones to manipulate situations to their own ends for food and reward. They have very good vision but, more importantly, a devious understanding of the world around them.

Crows raid nests for eggs and fledglings, eating many of our favourite songbirds. They are also known to eat small mammals, even bats and snakes on occasion, and being omnivores, they also eat seeds and grain, so they are serious pests and worthy of any shooter's quarry bag. You normally first spot a crow as it's leaving the ground or tree, because you've spooked it long before you were aware it was even there.

On one of my shoots, I can slowly drive right past a crow sitting on the ground or a fence post, and it won't even bat an eyelid, but as soon as the car comes to a standstill, it flies off. The odd one that might remain is gone when I extend my arm and point toward it, to mimic aiming a gun – they seem to know what that means. They don't like things being pointed at them and it's a strategy that clearly works to keep them alive.

You cannot really stalk crows – their eyesight is too good and they are simply too clever. You might get lucky and get the odd one, but its pot-luck really, so how do we outwit this formidable foe? Well, as with other corvids, their inquisitive nature is their undoing, and by far the best method for making serious inroads into their numbers is to decoy them with the addition of some culled carrion.

Pick your location based on a clear space to decoy to, and your ambush point in which to prepare your hide because you'll almost certainly need one. If I can, I'll also stretch the distance a little here to help me as much as possible with concealment, 30 yards is good. Open up the bait – a dead rabbit or grey squirrel – with its innards hanging out and place it belly up; placing a decoy on a fence or gate post nearby, and facing the bait, is a good way to get the decoy seen at distance and generate interest.

In terms of the hide, well, it needs to be top-drawer and, of course, summer woodland provides the best cover. I don't use a pop-up hide for crow shooting although they are ideal for shooting grey squirrels and woodpigeon, but try to use what is naturally available and engineer that into an effective hide. I might use some camo-leaf netting if I feel the need, but this will be complemented by as much natural foliage as I can locate and use. Place your hide just inside the outer tree line of the woodland – using the dark shadowy areas – and make this well in advance of the first day of shooting.

Use your laser rangefinder to learn the distance of certain markers; i.e., the fencing in the distance, the gates, any landmarks and so on. This will give you a good feel of the area around you and the compensation you might need to apply (hold over) if the incoming crows do not come straight onto the carrion, but land some small distance away, as they often do. That's not to suggest that you take the shot if they land 40 yards away, but it is important for the hunter to have a good knowledge of the space around them.

Ideally, let them approach the carrion and start eating. Now take the shot. A friend of mine has a kind of gun cradle attached to his shooting stick, in which he simply places his gun and leaves it set up on the carrion. He doesn't even have to undergo the additional movement of shouldering the gun as the crows come in, it is already set and he simply needs to move toward the gun allowing it to 'sit' into his shoulder, and only minor adjustments need to be made in order to place the crosshair in the right spot. This also means minimal movement is required to take the shot. He swears by it for crow shooting with an air rifle.

Carrion crows can be a problem all year round, although particularly at lambing time when they are notorious for attacking freshly born lambs and pecking at their eyes. I've heard some people argue that the crows are just trying to eat the protein in the afterbirth that the for pest control and the newborn lamb is coated in, though this fails to explain why lambs a few weeks old can still be vulnerable, not to mention the awful and stressful experience they must go through when being attached.

If you have permission from a sheep farmer to shoot on their land, make sure you offer your support around lambing time. They will be very grateful for the extra pair of eyes on site, and of course, for the crows being removed from the area. You might be present and able to scare the odd fox away as well; the slime coating that covers a newly-born lamb smells a great deal and does attract Charlie in from far and wide. Some professional fox shooters I know make their own 'mix' to mimic this smell, and

HUNTING: FEATHER   8

put it down in a field and watch through night-vision and thermal-imaging as the fox comes in from a considerable distance.

Like the woodpigeon, crows use 'sitty' trees, places from which they like to rest, watch and observe. Once these trees have been identified, young crows can be shot from them in the days and weeks following fledging. They have not yet fully developed that legendary awareness, and so you can take a few of them this way. Ambushing near these trees is also a good idea that can work well, but make sure that you're not spotted making your hide or putting the carrion out because that's a sure way of making them move on. Pick your times to be there and your times not to be seen there.

Rooks and Jackdaws

Like other corvids, rooks and jackdaws steal eggs and take carrion. Jackdaws are the smallest of the crow family, and both rooks and jackdaws differ from their larger crow brother in that they live in large groups. Although classed as a pest species, rooks do have some redeeming features for the farmer; at certain times of the year they eat leather jackets (crane-fly larvae), wireworms, earthworms, and grubs – thus benefitting crops. This has led to the view from some to leave them alone because these benefits can offset any shortcomings for the farmer. It is a judgment call, really. If the farmer or landowner wants them gone because they are over-populating the area and causing problems, then it is legitimate to control their numbers. However, if only present in small numbers it might be worth leaving them well alone.

Rooks and jackdaws can also be decoyed, but I often find it can be harder to get them to take to the decoys. They are creatures of habit and might have a favourite field or area at certain times of the year. Observing them will reveal this to you, so you know where to be and where to decoy. Rooks also like to feed until quite late and well into dusk time – basically capturing the last light or the day and returning to roost just before it gets dark.

Hitting the rookery and shooting the chicks as they get ready to fledge the nest is a common hunting practice. Rooks typically get ready to fledge the nest by the end of the second week in May, so do your research in the rookery to calculate the age of the chicks, when they are being fed by parents, etc., and get a feel for how things are in the rookery before you actually shoot. Do not shoot them when they are too young and are still in the nest, or just on the edge of it – it's not very sporting, and they will often just fall back into the nest, high in the tree canopy and out of reach.

Do you ever get the feeling you're being watched? Well, out in the woods and fields you often are being watched and from quite a distance away. Most corvids like to use trees to sit in and watch what is going on around them. They nearly always have the best seat in the house. It's close to impossible to stalk them so you'd best have a plan that involves a hide or being concealed and in position before they come to the trees.

As the chicks grow and become more confident over the days, they will move more and more to the outer edge of the branches getting ready to fledge, and that's when best to take them. Once you start hitting the young chicks, be ready for a deafening noise from the adults as they come swooping in. Rook chicks make the best rook pie, so again, as well as helping to control pests, you have a tasty meal ahead of you. Rooks have positive attributes and many hunters leave the chicks so that they can have a positive impact on the land. So, when shooting rooks, always try to be aware of the numbers you need to take and the numbers to leave in order to try to balance positive and negative effects. A very dry summer can lead to some good rook and jackdaw shooting. If there has been a period of sustained summer weather the soil can become overly hard and crusty – preventing their access to bugs and insects. The rain will soften things up again, but until then the rooks and jackdaws will need to find a substitute. I shoot on a number of estates that have poultry and pheasant feeders and these canny corvids can be resourceful in hitting these, particularly in the early morning. Watch for such changes in their behaviour and learn to capitalise on them.

Finally, for all types of ambush or hide shooting, I'd advise you to break cover rarely and try to remain hidden and leave the dead animals where they fall for as long as you can. Sometimes, this might not be possible, but when it is possible it's a good method to adopt. Dead pigeons can be added to your decoy pattern, and dead rabbits will be fine where they are for a while. Some exceptions might be on very hot days when you need to paunch them sooner rather than later, but I'd still advise leaving it under these circumstances to have as few 'cover-breaking' moments as possible. If the shooting is good, stay put.

9 Hunting: Things to Consider on Every Trip

CHALLENGING WEATHER AND WIND CONDITIONS

Weather – the ever-changing variable in the hunter's life. Sometimes it works with us, and sometimes against us. Strong winds will affect the trajectory of your pellet and you can certainly expect to miss 25- or 30-yard shots completely in strong crosswinds, without some consideration of the direction and strength of the wind. Indeed, extreme winds might suggest not shooting at all.

I have a basic rule: In bad conditions, curtail the distance at which you would take a shot on. The magnitude of this would be dependent on the severity of the wind or rain. Be disciplined about it when out hunting, and do not take on shots over a certain distance. Out to 25 yards, my .22 calibre guns are not that bothered by medium crosswinds or mild rain. Much beyond that and it is a gamble – one I will not take. Of course, some scope reticles have wind compensation marks on them that can be used, once well learned, but on the whole, if the wind is excessive I'll curtail the distance and compensate less.

In really high winds, I prefer to shoot in woodland rather than open fields because the outer trees provide a great source of shelter, and sometimes there is absolutely no noticeable wind or rain in the middle of the woodland, whilst it blows a gale around the perimeter. It can be a different world in the heart of the woods. The wind can also help you to get a lot closer because the animal might not hear you, and any noise you make competes with the wind howling through the tree canopies, through barns, etc, so the adverse conditions can be used to your advantage. On the one hand, you might need to curtail your distance for shots, but you can get closer in these conditions, so these factors tend to balance themselves out.

Sometimes it appears a futile and pointless exercise to go shooting in bad weather. It can seem like you are the only thing stupid enough to be out in the rain and wind, so it is not a timid approach to leave the guns at home on such days and curl up in front of the fire with a beer.

Rabbits, for instance, do not like the rain. I've heard it said that this is partly because they cannot hear predators approach due to the noise created by the falling rain hitting the ground, but who knows? That's not to say you won't see the odd one or two about, but you will not see them in the typical numbers. However, rabbits come out in droves soon after the rain – the grazing must taste better – and this is a good time to be in position ready to seize on the opportunity. So, if rabbits are the quarry of choice, going out in the rain can make sense, if you are trying to get into position for when the rain stops. Some of the best rabbit shooting can be had on a summer evening after a light shower, when the sun breaks through the clouds to generate warm, sunny patches on wet grass.

Grey squirrels are similar in that they will avoid the heavy rain unless it has been raining for a couple of days solid, in which case they will venture out for food. However, as with rabbits, their numbers are lower than would normally be the case. Bird species head for shelter in the woods or farm buildings and so this could be a good time to target those species and locations.

When thinking of the weather the real question is, how changeable is it likely to be? Is it going to bucket it down all evening, or is it expected to stop a couple of hours before sunset? The latter scenario would be ideal, so it is important to think about what the weather is doing now, but also what it is predicted to do in an hour or so, or when you plan to be in position. Of course, weather forecasts are notorious for their inaccuracy and I must confess to having to walk back to the car on many occasions in the middle of torrential downpours that were predicted to be brief, but persist longer than an unwelcome relative at Christmas. So much for trying to be clever about it. Nevertheless, being in position when the rain has been predicted to stop, and it does, can be a very productive time. It is a gamble, but don't be overly defeated by the fact that it's raining at 5pm because it might be a pleasant evening by 7pm – even more so if you're already in position and ready.

By now you will realise that effective hunting with airguns is not just a case of putting the crosshairs on the head of some critter and pulling the trigger. There is so much more going on, so much more to consider and so much more of which to be aware. Do not let that put you off – in fact, it is half the fun. There is no better feeling than when it all comes together in the field and your hunting bag starts filling up because of the successful application of well-thought-out principles and your know-how.

HUNTING: THINGS TO CONSIDER ON EVERY TRIP

DISTANCE TO TARGET

Estimating the distance from shooter to target is very important in hunting with airguns. For the larger calibres (.22), the pellet has a more curved trajectory. The smaller calibres (.177) travel faster, and so fly flatter for longer, but still provide a curved trajectory. In both cases, hunters need an understanding of distance, how it impacts on pellet trajectory, and how to compensate for this to ensure precision over distance. A 16 grain AA Field Diabolo .22 pellet, zeroed for 28 yards, will have dropped just less than 25mm (1 inch) by 35 yards, and by around 2 inches at 40 yards. The same pellet in .177, (8.40 grains) zeroed at the same distance will have dropped by less than half an inch at 35 yards, and less than 1 inch (0.86-inch to be exact) at 40 yards. Therefore, a good 'feel' for distance is an important skill for stalking quarry and accurate shooting.

Distance can be estimated in a number of ways; a laser rangefinder does it for you, but a true hunter needs some skill in this area without a rangefinder. Don't get me wrong, I own and now use a rangefinder, but I was estimating distances for 30 years before buying one. I'm good at visual estimations out to 35 yards, and accurate to about 2 yards – confirmed by many tests with the rangefinder. Sometimes, I try to imagine my zero distance in my head, or a distance I know, and then superimpose that onto what I'm looking at. For example, is that rabbit I can see actually further away than the length of my garden? Or, through research on my shooting permissions I will have previously stepped it out or lasered various positions relative to feeding or roosting positions, or the pigeons' favourite sitty tree. Sometimes, if you've done your research, you don't need to estimate distance – you know it exactly!

INCLINE AND DECLINE

The angle one is shooting at also impacts on shot placement. This is due to the differential effects of gravity on the pellet. When we zero the scope on our airgun, this is typically done when shooting parallel to the ground. Here, gravity has a particular effect on the pellet, where it is pulling from beneath it – and this is taken into account when the scope is being zeroed. However, the effects of gravity on a 25-yard shot parallel to the ground is very different to a similar shot at a 65-degree angle up into the trees. Therefore, your zero will not be 'spot on' and some form of compensation will be required in order to achieve the necessary placement of the shot.

It would not be prudent to give explicit advice on the degree of compensation because it will differ depending on many factors; shooting distance, angle, etc. This is why getting to know your combo and set-up is so important for hunting with airguns. I can say, though, that when shooting at targets inclined or declined relative to your position, some thought of the need to compensate must be given. A general rule of thumb is to aim lower when shooting at angles greater than 45 degrees. Try experimenting for yourself, by shooting at leaves or acorns at various heights on a tree and from various distances, to get a feel for the degree of compensation that you might require, for a given distance and a given inclination or declination. A good tip is to take a few practice shots once you're in position, before the pigeons fly into your intended ambush, if you think that angles are an issue and compensation might be needed.

Remember, when shooting at steep angles, some compensation might be needed in the POI. The degree of compensation is dependent on many factors, including distance and angle, and so some preliminary practice shots at leaves on the tree help the hunter to evaluate the degree of compensation required from their shooting position at various angles and distances.

HUNTING: THINGS TO CONSIDER ON EVERY TRIP

CHECKING THE ZERO

It is good practice to check the zero on the airgun before any shooting foray, just to be sure that everything is in order. One way to do this is merely to take a few test shots once you arrive at your shooting permission, just to ensure that nothing has crept off zero whilst the gun has been in transit, or for whatever reason. Find a target at your typical zero distance – a pebble, acorn, tree leaf, and simply take two or three shots. If all is well, you can have confidence in your zero.

The zero on a gun can alter for a variety of reasons. On old springers, scopes were well known for 'creeping' over time, due to recoil, although modern springers do not suffer from this as much, if at all, due to better quality mounts and arrestor pins that prevent creep. Vibration, knocking the scope or the end of the moderator can all impact on the gun's zero. Air temperature is another thing that affects the trajectory of the pellet. A gun zeroed in winter might not hold for summer, and could require adjustment, so to be absolutely sure, it is always prudent to take a couple of test shots at the start of every hunting trip.

10 Case Studies

SOME OF MY OWN HUNTING AND CONSERVATION PROJECTS

I am lucky to have the trust and support of a number of landowners who allow me to shoot pests and vermin on their property. To provide an illustrative context for the information contained within this book, to show the sorts of challenges that can be posed, and just some ways one could address them, I relate here some of the projects with which I am involved. I have no doubt that in some cases other methods would have equal merit, although what I cover here is what I know worked, and what continues to work, in these specific contexts.

STATELY ESTATE (I)

Squirrel project

I am deeply fortunate to have an excellent relationship with a family who own a stately home in the Lake District. The beautiful house is set in extensive grounds that consist of dense forest and woodland, as well as manicured sections and gardens adorned with exotic plants. There are many species of plants and trees in the grounds that require care and attention and represent a huge investment of time and money on the part of the owners – as well as having historical importance. The woodland was once home to our native red squirrel, but in recent years, the less welcome grey squirrel entered and populated the woodland, and until recently the reds had not been spotted for a long time. If grey squirrels become too numerous, the reds will simply stop breeding altogether and either move on, or die out in a given area.

A number of years ago, the owner asked me to shoot some grey squirrels that were pinching the food she was putting out on her window ledge, for the songbirds. I remember shooting a few near to the house before seeing no more, and then thought little more about it. Years later, it appears that they are back with a vengeance, and

CASE STUDIES 10

have a much stronger hold in the broader woodland. My good friend, Peter 'the squirrel man', lives nearby and he set up and directs the squirrel project here. He deserves all the credit for his magnificent efforts – I merely help out when I can and I am delighted to be part of it. Peter has set up some 19 feeders, or so, around this vast estate, and couples airgunning with occasional trapping. The feeders are placed approximately five feet from the ground and fixed to sturdy tree trunks. The strategy here is to have feeders in different sections or zones of the woodland, and to monitor activity on them. This can involve simply monitoring food levels in the feeders to see which ones are being targeted and used, or consulting trail-camera footage set on the feeders, which also helps to establish regular feeding times and routines.

The trick now is to get out into the woods before the squirrels come to feed, set up at a suitable distance, in a safe position and angle so as not to shoot the feeder itself if you miss the intended quarry, with good concealment – and wait. Luckily, there is a lot of excellent cover around to blend into, so one is not stuck for options. I typically pick my spot and ensure the line of sight is clear, with no branches and twigs in the path of the potential shot.

The next step is to set up the shooting stick so that it is steady, firm, and elevated correctly for a comfortable posture, orientated toward the feeder. If its autumn or winter time, I scan the bare tree canopies above me for movement; if it is summer, I'll remain largely fixated on the feeder because the foliage is too dense to see anything in the canopy.

Peter's main weapon of choice is an HW100 in .177 calibre, which he is very happy with and it has served him well on this project. Over recent years, around 600 grey squirrels have been culled in this extensive woodland. A record of the culls is kept; location, gender, additional notes, and this is stored in a database to establish an estimate of numbers and the efficacy of the methods. I'm pleased to say that there has been a noticeable drop in the numbers of greys (sightings and culls) so a definite impact has been made. However, you rarely get them all and the project keeps both of us busy.

The lessons from a project like this come from its sheer scale. The woodland is vast and a clear strategy of establishing feeding stations, which can also be moved around if we see no activity, and trapping are needed. Here, the airgunner plans an ambush based on established behavioural patterns of the quarry. It requires a holistic and a well-thought-out approach; feeders, trail-cams, traps, and more than one airgunner. Circumstance often favours the prepared mind!

ABOVE: *The view, known as the 'Gateway to Paradise', looking up the Eskdale valley. Eskdale is a recognised home to the increasingly rare red squirrel.*

LEFT: *I'm not the only hunter keeping a keen eye on things in the extensive woodlands of this amazing location.*

Squirrels are around all year, although it can be easier to see them in the autumn, winter, and early spring months when many of the trees will have lost their foliage. During this time, you can see them scurrying through the high canopy and branches often en route to your feeding station. This is useful and helpful because you can get a better feel of the ratio of the ones you've seen, versus the ones you've shot. In the middle of summer, this location can be like a dense tropical jungle in certain places, and it is very difficult to see the squirrels on the move. Your best bet in these situations is to monitor the feeding stations themselves and wait for the squirrels

CASE STUDIES 10

RIGHT: *A rare and very special sighting – a native wild red squirrel returning to this woodland due to the successful culling of the grey squirrel in this region.* PHOTO COURTESY OF PETER 'THE SQUIRREL MAN'. *The return of the red squirrel is a fragile one, that requires constant monitoring and support. This is what it's all about!*

to appear on them, and to couple this with the use of traps. Opportunistic shots in random places will be much more difficult in the middle of summer due to the increased density of foliage.

One approach not appropriate for this particular project is drey-poking. This method can be very effective for the shotgun user, but it is not really one for the airgun. Basically, it involves poking dreys with a pole, and shooters picking off the fleeing squirrels – hence the need for a shotgun. Drey-poking is not suitable because these woodlands contain many expensive trees and plants, which cannot be peppered with gunshot. The woods have some public footpaths and closing these down for drey-poking might prove expensive, both financially and in terms of time. In addition, with the fragile return of some red squirrels there is no way of knowing which species is living in the drey you are about to poke, and poking reds is simply not acceptable. One final reason is that despite a serious grey-squirrel problem, Peter and I have struggled to locate many of the dreys in the woodlands. I recently saw a squirrel running up a tree and disappearing into its hollow trunk and we now suspect that a lot of these squirrels are using hollow sections of trees as dreys, as opposed to the more typical twig-based dreys – so there is not much to poke! These limitations might not be important for other woodland, but for this project, poking the dreys is one method we cannot use with a clear conscience.

In the height of summer, woodland can be too dense to spot quarry in the trees, so the trick is to have feeders already established in these areas and just monitor those – for squirrels – or decoy the woodpigeons, crows, and magpies, to a clearing on the ground and ambush them there.

Rabbits

This is the same location as the squirrel project discussed above, but it's a different pest project. The same woodland has a rabbit problem and they are eating the expensive plants, making holes in manicured lawns and driving the gardeners crazy. The rabbits are focused in one main area that I'd estimate to be about 500 square yards, give or take a few yards, which has its advantages because the problem is quite focused and

CASE STUDIES 10

totally unlike the problem with grey squirrels. There is a host of warrens and different groups of rabbits dispersed within this area, which also encompasses the main tourist entrance to the property and a main driveway through the parkland to the house, and central area of the attraction. There are a few things that need to be considered with this particular pest problem.

The prime concern is the location of the rabbits. Tourists are free to roam the grounds and people are often coming and going well into the evening during the summer months. This means extra care needs to be taken to ensure that no one is nearby or can stray into your firing line. To improve safety, I also ensure that I do not shoot across paths and main walkways, rather position myself on the same side as the rabbit and shoot parallel to the path, if at all possible, although you need to have done your research to know where the rabbits typically emerge from. With such locations, unsocial hours are the best for shooting, so early morning forays and late-night lamping have proved to be very effective.

For mornings in the summer, I try to be on site from 4am and get into position. If I spook a few on my way to an ambush site, it's not a huge problem because they will be out again before I finish. For evening shooting, I like to get to that part of the estate early, park up and plan my attack. I do a quick check for people or quarry in the region, and then get myself into my first position and wait either for an opportunistic shot, or darkness. These days I use a Tactical Ledray 500 lamping light, which is basically the size of a cigar, sits on top of my scope and is capable of giving a brilliant 180-metre beam – more than enough for me to scan the environment as well as shoot with. However, I like to use the lamp on an intermediate brightness setting for actual shooting because this seems to spook fewer rabbits, and the layout of the various areas does not call for the full brightness setting. For this project I use no filters, just the white light.

At night it can be difficult to judge distance effectively because many distance cues are not available to help estimate it. Using an adjustable objective lens is not fast enough, and requires the lamp being on to inspect the results – telling every rabbit in the northern hemisphere exactly where you are! A laser rangefinder is useful, used with the lamp, but laborious to get out of the pocket for every shot. You can now purchase scope-mounted, laser rangefinders for night shooting – but these represent more expense and more kit mounted to the gun.

One useful strategy is to locate your common and preferred shooting locations, chosen in this case for safety and concealment, and from these, laser various landmarks in various directions – bins, signposts, markings on the tarmac, fencing, certain trees, etc – that represent certain distances; 20, 30, 40 yards. When the rabbits come out, you can judge their distance down the scope, relative to the known distances of the landmarks you've chosen and lasered previously. A good memory helps, but it is an effective method. You can also peg out your own distance markers, wooden stakes in the ground, rocks or whatever, which demarcate a given distance, from a position.

These rabbits were really easy to lamp when I started on them. They were not used to it and so did not perceive it as a threat and got very confused. In situations like this, many rabbits will run toward the light like a near-death experience! The trick here is not to over-lamp. Rabbits will learn those contingencies quickly, so keep your methods varied. I might lamp two nights in a row, then give it a rest for a while before resuming the method sometime later. Finally, on a permission like this one the guns are secured in the car by 9am, at the latest. Joe Bloggs does not need to see or know about me, and the grounds start filling up with employees and residents, so it's best to put the gun away and tuck into some bacon butties and a coffee down the on-site café.

Woodland

Grey squirrels, rats

For me, the beauty of the Eskdale valley is unsurpassed in Lakeland, and it is up against some pretty stiff competition for that accolade. A well-known local chap owns a couple of bits of land in the valley, and I shoot squirrels, rats and other pests for him on both of these. This friend is passionate about protecting the habitat of the red squirrel, where they have a stronghold further up the valley, but the greys are making their way up there and have been spotted in various places. A red squirrel with parapox has been reported in the vicinity of Forge Bridge, Eskdale (central valley), which is a stone's throw from important woodland areas home to the red squirrel. Sad times, but it underlies the importance of hitting the woodland in the valley hard, to help the smaller more vulnerable reds as much as we can.

When I first started shooting on these lands, it was crows and magpies that I landed the most, simply by chance and opportunity. These were also causing problems on this shoot. I saw no squirrels on my initial visits, although signs of their

CASE STUDIES | 10

The Western Lake District waking up. Hunting with air rifles often means early starts. Let's be honest, sometimes it's worth it for the stunning views alone.

presence were plentiful, so a feeder strategy was adopted and we waited to see if these would see any activity. It took a little less than a week, but then they did. Without a trail-cam back then, I was blind to feeding times so had to do it the old-fashioned way by sitting in ambush. Specific sessions were created; 6am–9am, 10am–12 noon, 4pm–6pm, and 6pm–8pm in the summer. These times were adhered to for a week and revealed that the squirrels on this land feed mid-morning –10am – at one end of the woods, and mid-afternoon – 4pm – at the other end. They might well be the same squirrels feeding twice with a certain routine (timetabling) or completely separate animals – it's not always easy to tell. There were not a lot of them in these woods, but enough to be a problem, and enough to justify making an effort to eradicate them. At the time of writing, one of these bits of woodland is now clear of grey squirrels; there have been no sightings, no camera images and no feeding for over a year, but this situation requires constant monitoring. The project in the other section of woodland is ongoing.

When trying to reduce the spread of the grey squirrel, it is important to hit as many localised woodlands as possible at the same time because they will use all of the woodland around them, including little 'satellite' places on their way toward the denser woodland where they might settle and breed. There are many small pockets of woodland dotted up the Eskdale valley, and some larger and more formidable forest areas in higher Eskdale, and it is just as important to hit the smaller woodland, which might contain smaller numbers.

Grey squirrels are cunning. Once you start hitting the squirrels in one area, some squirrels could move to another one nearby, and ideally, you hit them there as well, if you have permission for both sets of land. This is the optimal strategy. Otherwise, you could end up thinking a certain wood is empty of squirrels, only for them to

Squirrel feeders. Note the one in the picture on the left has chew marks on the Perspex window. These are likely left by mice or rats trying to get to the mix. Either way, not squirrels and not the intended quarry here. The solution? The feeder in the photo on the right has a very heavy lid, too heavy for very small critters. Only squirrels have the strength to lift this lid and hit my feed. If you're buying or making squirrel feeders of this type of design, make sure it has a robust, flip-up lid to prevent the non-intended species from getting in. Thanks to the chaps at West-Lakes Squirrel Initiative for making the feeder on the right.

CASE STUDIES   10

The ancient woodlands of the upper Eskdale Valley – home to the native and endangered red squirrel, but for how much longer?

return once you have moved on somewhere else. Being able to hit a number of regions is a far surer way of making a real impact on their numbers.

This land also has a rat problem. The rats have a particular taste for the corn-based poultry food that the landowner puts down for his hens, bantams, and chickens, which roam freely. In fact, the rats often rush out of the bushes, and even sit inside a small feeder that lies on the ground, within minutes of the food being put down. I saw this for myself one night, ratty zooming out of the undergrowth into the feeder, a brief pause, and then with lightning speed, back off into the undergrowth. Then another came, then another, and so on. This predicable behaviour was their undoing. Unbeknown to them, on this night I'd set myself up about 15 yards away in a perfect ambush position, and let the AA Field Diabolos rain down on them. I had not prepared any liquid food for them, so knew I needed to be fast to get them because their pause in the feeder was never more than a couple of seconds, but it was enough, in this case. Rats also learn fast. I culled quite a few on the poultry feeder with my first blat at them, but then nothing for the rest of the evening, nor the following one. Perhaps I'd managed to eradicate all the rats in that section, although I seriously doubted it. A return visit some two weeks later revealed that they had reverted to their old ways around the poultry feeder. A fatal error for many of them. The battle continues.

The poultry seed feeder on the ground. The rats emerge from the hole in the ground towards the top of the picture, to eat the food in the feeder. Many rats have been culled in this little region known humorously as 'Ratmageddon'.

Farm (1)

Rabbits

This shooting permission is one absolutely huge field. It has a hedgerow around three of the four boundary edges that can give good cover, and a wire fence around the fourth. It is more or less flat, with a large farm building at one side of it for sheep and cattle, it has some old, gravel car tracks running through it and at the far end, some sand dunes and then the beach. Sections of the field were riddled with rabbits and the farmer told me that he wanted them gone. 'Take them all,' he said.

An assessment of the project revealed that the challenge would be getting close to the rabbits once they were out because there is no cover away from the boundary. There were a number of approaches that could be used here, and the first thing to do was my research. Although I'd seen plenty of rabbits scampering around in the field on a number of occasions, I didn't know where they were emerging from or returning to, and I also needed to identify common feeding places.

Once I'd located the active warrens, the favoured rabbit runs through the grass, and feeding places, I was ready to make a serious impact on this pest population. One approach would be simply to sit in the hedge, near to where I know they emerged, and wait for the rabbits to pop out and pick them off one by one. The hedgerow would also help give me cover and allow me to optimise my camouflage. Another would be to place myself some 30 yards away from the hedge, although directly facing it. Here, I'd be out in the open field and need to keep low – prone. I like to place myself a good distance away, allowing the rabbits to move from the boundary hedge a little and come closer to me, so that the actual shooting distance would be more like 20 yards when the shot presented itself. The effectiveness of this method is increased more if the wind – if there is one – is blowing toward you and not the rabbits. Nothing wrong with either approach, though, both were used and produced results in the early days.

There was one more challenge that this land posed for my bunny project; the field is used quite freely by all members of the public and people go for long walks, walk their dogs, go to the dunes or the beach, or go fishing by cutting through the field. In the early days of this project, I might set myself up an hour or so before the rabbits emerge, watch them come out and wait for them to settle before taking the shot, only for some unleashed dog to come storming into the area, or loud groups of people to approach and scare everything within a two-mile radius for an hour or so. This would also happen repeatedly on lovely summer evenings, when lots of people wanted to be out and about. So, some early attempts were totally ruined, but the method used to address this was simple – early morning shooting and/or late evening lamping. Rabbits like to feed really early and late into the night, so this made sense. Indeed, lamping was particularly successful on this land.

The main entrance to the field was near some street lighting, and a few houses were dotted around that location just outside the field. This region was also well populated with rabbits. The street lighting permeated about 25 yards into the field before simply becoming a background feature, and things descended into darkness. The rabbits showed little interest in the lamp on the first night, probably due to the presence of the street lights nearby, and a healthy number were culled over the next few nights.

The next phase was not to become predictable and only rely on lamping, or lamp too much across successive nights. The rabbit population is now reduced by about 80% compared to what it was before I started, and I continue to vary the method to keep the rabbits guessing and keep things interesting. The size of the field and availability of car tracks means one can also have a friend drive around the perimeter, whilst you shoot from the passenger seat – a job well suited to a carbine gun, if you ever want to try this method.

Neighbouring fields, owned by someone else, provide a constant source of new rabbits that stray and set up home in this field. As I do not have permission for that other land, this prevents me from making an even bigger impact on the numbers because I can clearly see the warrens. Nevertheless, the ground does not move anywhere near the degree it once did, and maintaining this state of affairs takes constant attention.

Farm (II)

Rabbits

This permission is a smallholding farm containing a number of old, stone outbuildings, pens and sheds, and a couple of fields, one of which is quite large. The pests of interest are rabbits and rooks – a farm nearby has a rookery and a few fly on to this causing all sorts of mischief. The landowner wanted the rabbits dealt with as the primary job, but also told me that some rooks roost in the high walls of the outbuildings and are causing problems on the land more generally, so he asked if I could take care of that, as well. 'Sure thing,' I said. 'My pleasure!"

So, my research was to chat to the farmer and the family about when and where the rabbits were being seen around the farm itself. A few spots were mentioned more than once, so these hotspots seemed a good place to concentrate initial efforts. I carried out a quick survey of the farm buildings, so that I could establish the quietest and quickest way to navigate around the farm and explore the best ambush locations for launching my efforts. Lots of nice options were available and plenty within 20–25 yards of rabbit sightings – I lasered and stepped out various locations. I could see that these rabbits hadn't been shot at before and were out feeding at all times of the day, so once my research was done, I decided to return home and plan my approach for the next day, which would be an early start and a memorable one.

CASE STUDIES 10

It was late July, and I arrived on site at around 4.30am, just as it was getting light. I had both PCPs in the car, but decided on the S410K, loaded the magazine into the gun and also took a shooting stick – my Primos Tripod Trigger Stick – which I had just purchased and was eager to see how it performed in the field. I entered the first, long, narrow barn and noticed that the door at the far end of it had been left ajar for me from the night before. I knew that the door led to a rabbit 'hot-spot', 90 degrees to the left once I'd passed through the door, which was on a hinge that left a gap of about six-inches-wide running the full length of the door. I could see through this gap clearly, and there was lots of room to poke the barrel of the gun through, so rather than walk through the open door and physically enter this courtyard area, I used the gap between the door and frame to scan the area.

Sure enough, I spotted three full-sized rabbits nibbling about 20 yards away. I released the legs on the trigger stick, dropped them down smoothly and quickly, spaced them out into a tripod configuration. Then I placed the S410K onto the stick, adjusted the height and centred the crosshair on a rabbit head, anterior to, but near the base of the ear for a classic side-on head shot. Thwack! A clean head shot and bunny humanely dispatched. The rabbit rolled over dead – no drama. The other two rabbits stayed put and were totally unconcerned by what had just taken place, or the demise of their fellow bunny. I chambered a second AA Field Diabolo pellet and the next bunny was done within a few seconds – PCPs allow for the rapid chambering of a new round, and contexts like this allow you to capitalise.

The last rabbit stopped nibbling for a few seconds, sat up and had a look around, but then just relaxed back into it and carried on feeding. Bang! – third one down. I will always remember this because I'd bagged three rabbits, in reasonable proximity to each other, in a very short time frame, all clean head shots and humane kills, and I hadn't really entered the land yet – I was still in the first barn! An example of the effectiveness of a multi-shot, sound-moderated PCP, if you ever needed one.

The main challenge from this land is the big field. It is as flat as a snooker table and close to the sea, so it experiences a lot of wind. In addition, only one of the four boundaries surrounding the field consists of a hedgerow to hide in, or to provide shadows to stick to in the evening. All the other boundaries are of wire fence, giving no concealment at all. The bunnies that stray into the farm buildings area are easy to pick off, but the ones that remain in the big field require other approaches in order to get close. On the whole, I've used the same strategy as that outlined for the large field permission discussed above; i.e., sitting in the hedge, facing the warrens from

35 yards away, or lamping, etc., with equally pleasing effectiveness, although the wind at this particular site makes me ever-conscious of distance so I try to keep things close, if possible. Sticking to the shadows cast into the field, whilst away from the cover of the hedgerow has also proved effective on this land. The rabbits often chase the sunny patches. The hunter stays in the shade.

Stately Estate (II)

Rabbits and grey squirrels

This project is a humble one – not very extensive in terms of acreage, but it does contain a very pleasant small woodland area that encompasses a rather nice Grade II listed manor house, surrounded by manicured lawns and some ornate flower and herb gardens. This project began with observation sessions to determine which species were present, where they were and what times they were out and about feeding or running around.

The approach to the grey squirrels was an optimised feeder-based approach, where a single feeder was established and trail cams placed on them, then feeding times were discovered and ambush sites set up. This proved to be very effective in this case; in under 16-months, 66 grey squirrels were humanely removed, and sightings now would suggest that only one or two are present in this area, which is a significant improvement since the start of the project.

There were a couple of rabbit hot spots on the main house lawn, so these were targeted and the rabbits removed fairly simply. It was difficult to get close to the rabbits when they were located in the middle of the lawn, so a camo-leaf blind was set up, I perched myself behind it and waited for them to emerge. This was very effective.

In other instances, I had to draw upon my longer-range shooting and took a number of bunnies in the region of 37 yards. It's nice to be able to call upon those skills when required, although ideally, I do prefer to stalk the distance down when possible. Although I shot most of the rabbits here, I did not get them all. Despite this I have not seen a rabbit on this land for a couple of years now. Perhaps foxes or raptors are responsible, perhaps RHD, who knows, but the rabbit problem has now been managed and resolved.

CASE STUDIES   10

A FAREWELL, THANK YOU AND HAPPY HUNTING

Well, we are now at the end of our journey together and I would like to finish this book by thanking you, the reader, for taking the time to read and digest my thoughts and ramblings. I hope you found it useful and helpful. My intention with this volume was to provide a primer, a guide to hunting with air rifles that was accessible to all. As well as covering tips and methods, I've also tried to share the broader aspects of hunting, such as how enriching being out in the countryside can be. There might be material in the book you disagree with, or you might think there is a better way to do things, and I welcome such thoughts because I am of the firm belief that we all learn more through discussion.

I've tried to present information as objectively as possible and be very clear when discussing my own personal subjective thoughts. To me this book is a guide to inform the reader's own decisions when hunting with airguns. It is not a concrete 'rule book' – such a thing would be ridiculous. I do not believe in saying 'this is exactly how it needs to be done', but merely provide principles that any hunter can adopt and adapt to their own situations, and in so doing, develop new and effective applications. I look forward to reading those developments and adaptations in the future. I've never claimed to be the best hunter, shot, or fieldsman – just a competent one, always looking to improve and learn.

I have enjoyed writing this book and putting my thoughts, feelings and expertise down on paper. I would also like to thank my wife for encouraging me to start this book and get my knowledge – for what it's worth – down on paper. My late paternal grandfather was a true Dalesman and a very accomplished fisherman of salmon and trout in the rivers of Eskdale. He knew the rivers well, the productive pools, the nooks and crannies … and they all had names, but much of this knowledge has now been lost and forgotten. Sadly, he never wrote down any of his knowledge or experiences and took them all with him to the grave – shame. I hope my humble offering here goes some way to providing recompense on behalf of a family of hunters and fieldsmen.

As I write this and bid you farewell, our two cats, Buffy and Brian, are curled up in their beds near a cracking log open fire on a late winter evening, keeping me company as they have done throughout the writing of these chapters. Formidable hunters of house bugs themselves, I hope they approve of the result.

Happy hunting!

10 THE AIRGUNNER'S COMPANION

After the job for the day is done, the guns wiped down and secured, time to crack out a cool one, enjoy the sunset and think about the ones that got away!

> *'We love our wild animals ... we study them; we watch them, we care for them, we make sure that they live and thrive and yet we shoot them ... it is a strange knife edge, a strange dichotomy, but that's hunting for you. You have to love the animals and yet kill them and nobody who is against hunting has ever managed to understand that – and the funny thing is, nobody who likes hunting has ever managed to understand that either.'*
>
> John 'The Hunter' Darling

Acknowledgements

There are many people I would like to thank and acknowledge for their help, time and input in supporting me and my hunting interests over many years. I would like to give a huge thank you to my ever-tolerant wife for her constant support and encouragement. I would like to thank, Peter and Iona Frost-Pennington, Ronnie and Judy Phizacalea, George, Lynn and John Tyson, Jimmy Craghill, Terry Pitts, Colin and Marjorie Hall, Gavin Lonsdale, and David, Claire, Chris, and Peter Middleton for all their support. I would like to thank the ever-colourful Murray Wilson and Martin Clapp for long chats about shooting all formats of guns and how to do it properly. I'd like to thank Peter 'the squirrel man' for his discussions about the grey squirrel project in West Cumbria, on land we both shoot together. I would also like to thank the members of the Sedbergh Red Squirrel Group and the West-Lakes Squirrel Initiative (WSLI) who do an excellent job of keeping on top of the grey squirrel invasion in Lakeland and help to support me with feed and feeders. I'd like to acknowledge a childhood friend, Simon Lawson, from Bootle village in Cumbria, my fellow airgunner in the early years when HW80s and Theoben Siroccos ruled the world – those were happy days. I haven't seen Simon in over 25 years, but writing this book has made me reflect on all the airgun experiences I have enjoyed.

Thanks are also due to Mike 'Cloverleaf' Rudge for tune-ups on my Air Arms Pre-Charged Pneumatics (PCPs) to ensure that they sing as sweetly as they were intended to – thanks for everything Mike! Thanks also to Tony Wall and all at Sandwell Field Sports (Birmingham) for constant advice, all the cups of coffee, and the occasional pork pie. I always come away with a smile on my face and having learned something new – even when I only popped in for pellets!

Finally, thanks to two men who had a big influence on me taking up airgunning in the first place. First, my late father who, once upon a time, could shoot rabbits in his sleep and set me on my path of humane hunting. I will always remember the bath full of rabbits when he had shot so many he had nowhere to put them. He did the same once with mackerel, but that's another story! Thanks for everything, Dad. Secondly, to the late, great, John 'The Hunter' Darling. John (or JD as he was known) wrote for airgun magazines back in the day when tuned spring power ruled

THE AIRGUNNER'S COMPANION

the airgun world. It would not be an exaggeration to call him an icon in the airgun community. His experience was inspirational and his articles more than educational. I will always remember being a young schoolboy, rushing home to read every month's instalment of *'The Hunter'* in *Air Gunner* magazine. As the old saying goes, *'true immortality is having lived a life worth being remembered for'*, and I remember his writings and teachings with great fondness. Thanks JD, your teachings go with me on every hunting foray, although my mistakes remain my own.

DISCLAIMER

Throughout this book, I mention certain brands, manufacturers and associations. It is important that the reader knows I am not in receipt of any financial incentive to mention any of these products. My recommendations are based purely on my experience. My views are as objective as they can be, based on evidence and observation from years of hunting with airguns and being a part of projects that demand results. I'm experienced enough to have made many pointless purchases and a few silly mistakes along the way. I hope that by reading this book you won't have to make those same mistakes – although you're more than welcome to make your own!

Index

A

adjustable objective lenses (A/O) 50, 50, 57, 58, 189
advantages, of airguns 17–18, 27, 28–29, 32
Air Arms (AAs) 13, 31–32, 37, 52, 52, 63
   case studies with 67, 193, 197
   guns
      S410 Classic 32, 34, 37, 57, 65, 66–67, 67, 68
      S410K 'Tiger' 54, 59, 65–67, 65, 66, 70, 197
      TX200 HC 'T-Rex' 31, 63–64, 63
   pellets 69
      Field Diabolos 44, 45, 48, 54, 69, 181
air cylinders 32, 37
air pressure 37, 42, 57, 59
AirgunForum (AGF) 66
ambushing 17, 120–123, 145–146, 155, 178
   see also camouflage; feeding (baiting)
   equipment for 34, 67, 69, 88, 89
ammunition *see* pellets
angles *see* trajectories
apparel 93–98
   see also camouflage
army-surplus clothing 95

B

backpacks
bags 32, 89, 90
baiting *see* feeding (baiting)
ballistic coefficient (BC) 44, 47
'barrel crack' 52
batteries 20, 91–92, 130
bench rests 56–57, 57, 58, 61–62
'biological motion' 95, 110, 114, 156
bipods 20, 87–88, 90, 123
bird species *see* blue jays; crows; doves, collared; jackdaws; magpies; pigeons, feral; rooks; woodpigeons

blue jays 19, 172–173
boots 98, 128
brain shots 71, 72–74, 75, 75
break-barrels 31
British Association for Shooting and Conservation (BASC) 25, 26, 79
broken rhythm 148–150
Browning Trail Cameras 102
Bushnell 48, 102
butt-plates 34, 58, 67

C

cabinets 25
calibres 22, 32, 44
   .177 22, 35–36, 45, 53, 181
   .22 35–36, 48, 54, 55, 91
      and muzzle energy 21, 22
      and pellets 44–45, 181
cameras, surveillance 101–102, 143–144, 144
camo-netting 96, 99–101, 100, 103, 111, 108, 134
camouflage 79, 93–98, 107–115, 111, 128, 146, 170
   see also camo-netting
   for guns 114–115
canter 58, 61, 76–77, 119
carbines 22, 30, 32, 59, 63, 64–65, 69, 196
carrion, use of 175, 176, 177
Chairgun (Hawke Optics) 44, 54, 55, 56, 61
cheekpieces 59, 68, 76
chronographs 24, 24, 32, 37, 38, 46, 66
cleaning and maintenance
   feeder 141
   gun 40, 46, 47, 103
   pellets 46
'combos' (gun/scope/pellets) 53–55, 62–70
competition shooting 19, 22, 35, 46, 76
compressed air 28, 46
computer programmes 44, 55, 62

Chairgun 44, 54, 55, 56, 61
concealment 107–115, 111, 112, 113, 114, 120, 121
  see camo-netting; camouflage apparel
corvids see blue-jays; crows; jackdaws; magpies; rooks
crows 19, 114, 152, 175–177
  use of baiting and decoys 102, 134, 146, 148, 188
  use of camouflage 94, 108, 126
  use of hides 101
culling, of vermin 25, 72, 79, 158, 159, 163, 187
  see also humane dispatch
custom air rifles 20, 39–42, 68

D

decline 181–182
decoys 73, 82, 102–103, 102, 125, 146–148
  alongside other strategies 99, 101, 121, 134
  corvids 173, 174, 175, 177, 188
  pigeons and doves 169, 170, 171, 172, 178, 188
Deerhunter 96
diabolo pellets 44, 47
  Field Diabolos 44, 45, 48, 54, 69, 181
disadvantages, of airguns 18–19, 27, 29
dispersion, of pellets 22, 27, 36, 43–44, 47, 53, 69–70
disposal, of carcasses 80, 152
distance judgement 18, 91, 129, 181
  and stalking 115, 116
dive bottles 29, 32
domed (round-headed) pellets 44, 47, 48
doves, collared 19, 106, 130, 151–152, 171–172
dreys 124, 135, 137, 141–142, 159–160, 159
  drey-poking 187–188

E

eating quarry 17–18, 169
paunching and gutting 84, 85, 134, 150–151, 178
EKA 84, 85, 86
embodiment 33
energy-limited airguns 19
energy limits, UK 22
estates 184–190, 198

F

farmyard shooting 17, 36, 89, 116–117, 122, 128–130
  birds 171, 172
  case studies 194–198
  gaining permissions for 79–80
feeding (baiting) 25, 82, 121, 133–134
  carrion, use of 175, 176, 177
  setting up stations 101, 134–146, 139, 140, 157, 160, 162–163
    case studies 185, 192, 193–194
fettling (custom) air rifles 20, 39–42, 68
fines 25
Firearms Certificate (FAC) 24, 45
first-aid kits 104
fleas 151, 157
footwear 98, 128
freezers 103

G

game species *see also* pheasants
Garlands 96
Gary Cane Gun Stocks 68
gas-ram guns 31, 33
general licences 25–26, 169
ghillie suits 96, 99
grains (weights), pellets 35, 36, 44
gun shops 32, 39, 42
gutting 85, 134, 150–151

H

H&N Baracuda Hunter Extreme 44
hares 26
Harkila 96, 98
Hawke Optics 48, 54, 55, 56
  Chairgun 44, 54, 55, 56, 61
heart shots 72, 74–75
heat sensors (thermal spotters) 93
Helle 84, 85
hides 82, 99–101, 100, 103, 108, 122, 171
  guns for 65, 69
  netting 96, 99–101, 100, 103, 111, 108, 134

INDEX

placement 109, 124, 130, 147, 148, 175, 176
humane dispatch 19, 21, 30–31, 35, 43, 75
   see also point of impact (POI)
hunting laws, UK 19, 22, 23, 24–26, 30–34, 87
HW (Wiehrauch) 31–32, 52

I

incline 171, 181–182
insurance 26, 79

J

jackdaws 19, 128, 129, 177–178
JSB Exact Jumbos 44, 45, 48, 70

K

knives 84–87, 85

L

lamping 20, 23, 49, 82, 94, 130–132
   kits and night vision 91–93, 92
   rabbits 189, 195–196, 198
   rats 133, 168
land, boundaries 79, 81–82
land-management 154
landowners 23, 26, 79–81, 82–83
laser rangefinders 20, 91, 129, 181
laws, UK 19, 22, 23, 24–26, 30–34, 87
lenses *see* objective lenses
leptospirosis 166
licences 25–26, 169
lube 46, 47
Lyme disease 158

M

magazines 28, 33, 47, 47, 66
magnification (sights) 48, 49, 50, 51, 55, 56, 58, 62
magpies 19, 122, 152, 173–175, 174
   baiting 134
   decoys 102, 103, 146, 172, 188
   nests 159, 160
meetings, with landowners 79
mimicry, of animal noises 132, 174
mink 13, 19, 81, 163–166

moderators 17, 20, 28, 51–52, 67, 183
Mora Knives 86
Mossy Oak 95
MTC Optics 48
multi-shots 28, 32, 33, 47, 197
muzzle energy 21, 22, 24–25, 32, 40, 46, 53, 64, 115
   see also chronographs
myths, surrounding airguns 21–23
myxomatosis 156–157

N

Napier of London 90, 96
nests 135, 160, 164, 172, 175
   see also dreys; warrens
netting, camouflage 96, 99–101, 100, 103, 111, 108, 134
night shooting 23, 23, 93, 128, 189
   see also lamping; night vision (NV)
night vision (NV) 20, 91–93, 133, 150, 156, 168, 177
Nikko-Stirling 48
Nikon 48
noise, reduction of 96, 111, 119, 125, 127
non-Fire Arms Certificate (non-FAC) 21, 24

O

objective lenses 48–49, 66
   adjustable (A/O) 50, 50, 57, 58, 189
observation 105–107, 124, 130
Opinel 86
organised shoots 16

P

parabolic trajectories 53, 54
parallax error 49–51, 58, 59
parapoxvirus 158, 190
parasites 151
passive infrared (PIR)-enables cameras 143
paunching 84, 85, 150–151, 178
pellets 17, 22, 32, 42–47, 47, 48
   choice of 18, 20, 53, 69–70
   lubrication of 46, 47
   and muzzle energy 25, 32, 67
      see also calibres
   performance of 54, 55, 69, 70, 70

THE AIRGUNNER'S COMPANION

see also Chairgun (Hawke Optics); trajectories
and point of impact (POI) 18, 70–75
  storage of 25
  weights (grains) 35, 36, 44
penalties 25
permissions 26, 79–81
  assessing boundaries 81–82
pest control 25, 72, 79, 158, 159, 163, 187
pest species *see* birds; mink; rabbits; rats; squirrels, grey
pheasants 16, 81
pigeons, feral 19, 101, 129, 172
pistol grips 33, 68, 78
pneumatics *see* pre-charged pneumatics (PCPs)
poaching 23
point of impact (POI) 18, 70–75
pointed pellets 43–44
poisons 17, 167
'power curve' 37, 66
practice *see* target shooting
pre-charged pneumatics (PCPs) 20, 28–30, 33, 30, 37–39, 40–41
  brands and costs 31–32, 65
  and pellets 44–45
  sound moderators 51
  zeroed distance 55, 59
Primos Hunting 87, 88, 197
protected species 27
Pulsar 93
pumps 29, 32

R

Rabbit Haemorrhagic Disease (RHD / RHD-2) 157
rabbits 19, 21, 26, 153–157, 153, 157
  see also warrens
  ambushing 122, 123, 124
  behaviours 154, 155, 156, 180
  case studies on farmland 194–198
  case studies on stately estate 188–190, 198
  handling and preparing carcasses 84–86, 85, 150–151
  observation of 82, 106–107, 124
  point of impact (POI) for 72, 73, 74–75
  stalking 117–119, 149

use of baiting and decoys 103, 134
use of camouflage 93, 94, 98, 108, 110, 114, 126
use of lamping and night vision 23, 93, 130, 131–132
rake angles 33, 78
rangefinders, laser 20, 91, 129, 181
rats 17, 19, 133, 152, 166–168
  case studies on stately estate 190–194, 194
  use of lamping and night vision 93, 130
ravens 26
Realtree 95, 96, 97
refreshments 104
Registered Firearms Dealers (RFD) 42
reticles 48, 49, 50, 51, 55, 56, 58, 62, 125
rooks 19, 26, 101, 128, 129, 158, 177–178
round-headed pellets 44, 47, 48
rucksacks 90
Rudge, Mike 66–67

S

Sandwell Field Sports, Birmingham 39
scopes (telescopic sights) 20, 31, 32, 48–51, 50, 55
seats 89–90, 89
second-hand airguns 31
Seeland 96
shared permissions 80
sharpening, knives 84–86
shooting sticks 61, 87–88, 87, 89, 146, 167
shotguns 16–17, 18, 80, 101
shots (ammunition) 17
sights (scope)
  see also zeroed distance
  fibre-optics 20
  open barrel 20
  telescopic 20, 31, 32, 48–51, 50, 55
  zeroing rifles 58
silencers (sound moderators) 20, 51–52
single-shots 32, 33
skinning 85, 151
sling and swivels (straps) 32, 64
sound moderators 20, 51–52
spring-powered guns (springers) 20, 27–28, 28, 29, 33
  brands and costs 31, 63, 63

sound moderators 51–52
  tuning 40
SpyPoint 102
squirrels, grey 19, 27, 120, 122, 158–163, 158
  see also dreys
  behaviours 124, 145–146, 158–159, 180
  case studies in woodland 190–194
  case studies on stately estate 184–188, 198
  point of impact (POI) for 72, 73–74
  use of baiting and decoys 103, 133–134
  use of camouflage 96, 98, 99, 100, 112, 126
  use of feeders 101, 134–146, 139, 140, 160, 162
  use of thermal spotters 93
squirrels, red 26, 144, 158, 187
stalking 17, 115–120, 150, 155
  equipment for 65, 69, 94, 96, 98
  in woodland 123, 125, 126, 160
stately estates 184–190, 198
stoats 19, 163, 164
stocks 20, 33, 58–59, 114
  grips on 78
thumbhole stocks 34, 34, 58, 67
  walnut 39, 63, 63, 68
storage
  of guns and pellets 25, 46, 47
  of knives 87
  of quarry 89, 90
straps 32, 64
supports 57, 57
  see also bench rests
surveillance cameras 101–102, 143–144, 144
'sweet spots' 37–38, 38, 58–59

T

target shooting 19, 22, 35, 40, 60, 64, 65, 69–70, 76
  see also competition shooting
telescopic sights 20, 31, 32, 48–51, 50, 55
thermal spotters 93
throat shots 72, 73, 75
thumbhole stocks 34, 34, 58, 67
ticks 123, 158
'Tiger' (AA S410K) 54, 59, 65–67, 65, 66, 70, 197
trail cameras 101–102, 143–144, 144
trajectories 18, 35–36, 43, 44, 62, 125, 129, 181
  parabolic 53, 54
'T-Rex' (AA TX200 HC) 31, 63–64, 63
trigger sticks 87, 88, 197
triggers 20, 33–34, 60–61, 60, 64, 67
tuned (custom) air rifles 20, 39–42, 68

U

under-levers 13, 28, 31, 63

V

Venom Arms Company 39, 41
vermin control 25, 72, 79, 158, 159, 163, 187
vermin species *see* birds; mink; rabbits; rats; squirrels, grey

W

warrens 106, 123, 124, 153–154, 195
weasels 19, 163, 164
weather, effect on shots 72–73, 179–180
weather-proof clothing 97
Webley & Scott 62
Weil's disease 166
Wiehrauch (HW) 31–32, 52
wind conditions 179–180
woodland hunting 123–127, 190–194
  see also camouflage
  equipment for 52, 65, 65, 69, 93
  feeders in 135–146, 139, 140
woodpigeons 17, 19, 118, 169–171, 170
  behaviours 122, 124, 128, 129, 134, 146–148
  handling carcasses 151–152
  observation of 106, 107, 124
  point of impact (POI) for 73, 74, 75
  use of baiting and decoys 102, 134, 146–148, 188
  use of camouflage 94, 99, 108, 126
  use of hides 99, 176

Z

zeroed distance 38, 39, 45, 53–62, 183